CW01045262

Cork Strolls

Gregory and Audrey Bracken, from County Kildare, are a brother and sister with a love of travel. Between them, they have published guides to Dublin, London, Paris, Bangkok, Hong Kong and others. Gregory has a PhD in Architecture and is Assistant Professor at the Technical University of Delft in the Netherlands. Audrey has a BA in English and Classics and, after a career in publishing and marketing in London and New York, now lives in Dublin with her two children.

Stay up-to-date with the authors at:

 @irelandstrolls

 @irelandstrolls

Also by Gregory and Audrey Bracken

Dublin Strolls

Colour Dublin

Kuala Lumpur: A Walking Tour

Praise for *Dublin Strolls*

Draws attention to the lesser-known points of interest ... Thanks to Gregory and Audrey Bracken, you'll never look at Dublin the same way again. Irish Examiner

Quirky and interesting ... an engaging guide to scour rather than flick through. The Irish Times

Uncovers some fascinating – and forgotten – histories. Irish Independent

An enlightening and inspiring guidebook. The Herald

Has the lovely tone of a knowledgeable friend and includes practical advice. www.dublininquirer.com

Boasts easy-to-follow walks, architectural insights and coverage of landmark buildings, and a host of little-known facts about Dublin's structures and streets. The Irish Post

Cork Strolls

Exploring Cork's Architectural Treasures

Gregory and Audrey Bracken

The Collins Press

To Mum, with all our love

FIRST PUBLISHED IN 2018 BY
The Collins Press
West Link Park
Doughcloyne
Wilton
Cork
T12 N5EF
Ireland

Reprinted 2018

Paperback ISBN: 978-1-84889-342-9

Design and typesetting by Studio 10 Design
Typeset in Amasis
Printed in Malta by Gutenberg Press Limited

—∞∞∞—

CONTENTS

Acknowledgments

Thanks, as always, to Robert Cortlever, without whom none of these books would be possible. A special thanks goes to Marcin Dabrowski for your great suggestions about the maps. Thank you, too, to John Cabell, for giving your time to the project, and to Karin and Geert Wiegersma for the all-important time spent in Lesvaux every summer, which is where so much of the work on these books gets started, and done. And finally, we'd like to say a very special thank you to Sandra O'Connell at the RIAI for your wonderful support, advice and help: it's very much appreciated.

INTRODUCTION

ORK'S COAT OF ARMS shows a ship sailing between two towers and has the motto *Statio bene fida carinis* (a safe harbour for ships). This is because Cork has one of the world's finest natural harbours. The harbour has six islands: Great, Little, Fota, Spike, Haulbowline and Rocky. Cork itself was established on another island, at the point where the River Lee meets the harbour – and it takes its name from those marshes (*corcaigh* is Irish for marsh).

St Finbarr founded a monastery here in the early seventh century but there was already a large Celtic habitation on the north bank of the river. Then Vikings began to invade from Norway in the ninth century, and eventually settled down peacefully. More Viking invaders came, this time from Denmark, and they, too, eventually settled. These various communities, the Vikings and the Irish, seem to have got along pretty well because there is evidence of trade – wine and salt being imported, and wool and animal hides exported. These were the beginnings of a long tradition of trading in the city.

IRELAND

Dublin

Cork

The Anglo-Normans arrived in Ireland in 1169 and began to colonise. The Danes and Irish put up a fight but were eventually defeated. Henry II granted the city its first charter in 1185, and Cork had its first mayor, Richard Wine, in 1273. The Anglo-Normans built a stone wall around the old Danish settlement, developing it into a prosperous town (you can still see some of these city walls in Bishop Lucey Park on

Southgate Bridge with St Fin Barre's Cathedral

Grand Parade). The medieval city ran from Northgate Bridge to Southgate Bridge via the main thoroughfare of North and South Main Streets. It was home to about 2,000 people and continued to thrive as a trading centre, with a dozen or so merchant families dominating the city's commercial life. The Anglo-Normans brought their own system of government and law; they also attracted the great monastic orders, Augustines, Dominicans and Franciscans, all of whom built abbeys and churches (the ruined tower of Red Abbey on the south side of the city is one of the few visible reminders of this time). English colonisation continued throughout the medieval period and into the Renaissance, with the native Irish lords losing lands to the new settlers (including people like the explorer Sir Walter Raleigh and the poet Sir Edmund Spenser, who got married in St Fin Barre's Cathedral).

Eventually the native Irish rebelled against these incursions, and an army led by the northern chiefs O'Neill and O'Donnell, who enlisted Spanish help, engaged the English in battle at Kinsale in 1601. They were defeated and fled (an event known as the Flight

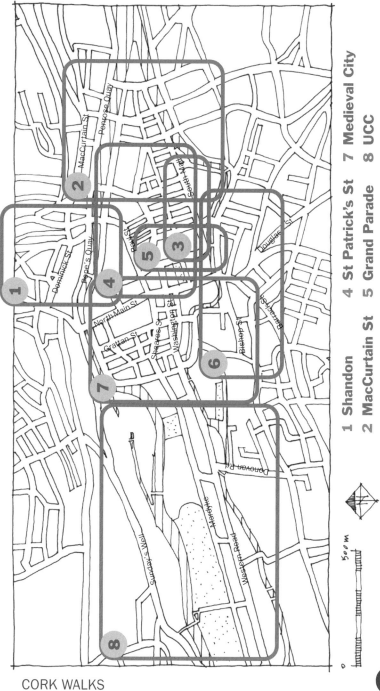

CORK WALKS

1 Shandon   4 St Patrick's St   7 Medieval City

2 MacCurtain St   5 Grand Parade   8 UCC

3 South Mall   6 Holy Trinity

of the Earls). This changed the course of Irish history. The English way of life replaced the traditional Irish one, dealing a serious blow to Irish culture, heritage and language. (This was revived towards the end of the nineteenth century in a movement spearheaded, oddly enough, by the Anglo-Irish descendants of these erstwhile colonial invaders.) The seventeenth century was a hard time for native Irish Catholics. Cromwell campaigned against them in the 1640s, and then later in the century the 1690 Siege of Cork reduced much of the city to rubble. This was part of William III's campaign to wrest the throne from his father-in-law, James II (a Catholic), which he did through a series of military campaigns in Ireland, including the Siege of Derry and the Battle of the Boyne, also in 1690. Hostilities ended with the Treaty of Limerick the following year, after which Irish Catholics lived under very strict controls known as the Penal Laws. Many were expelled from Cork, and forced to surrender their property. Yet despite this, trade continued to flourish and the city's first bank opened in 1680. But the city's commercial life was definitely in the hands of the Protestants, who received a boost when French Huguenots began to arrive in 1685. These refugees, fleeing religious persecution in France, settled around Paul Street and French Church Street, marshy islands that were being reclaimed and added to the city as the old medieval heart expanded eastwards.

Cork's wealth continued to be based on trade, mainly the export of butter, beef, pork and animal hides. The Cork Butter Market opened in 1769 and became hugely successful, exporting butter to Great Britain and Europe and even as far away as North America and the Caribbean. Much of the city had to be rebuilt after the 1690 siege, and many of the city's fine churches and cathedrals date from this time. This was also when the quays (pronounced 'kays' in Cork)

DID YOU KNOW?

Cork gave the Freedom of the City to Dean Jonathan Swift in 1736.

were built, and when the great streets of St Patrick's Street and Grand Parade were developed. Originally waterways, these were filled in and became fashionable residential and commercial districts in the eighteenth century. Cork may never have developed the gracious Georgian squares that are such a feature of Dublin's streetscape, probably because it was not ringed by great estates like Dublin (or London), and there were no landowning families like the Fitzwilliams or Gardiners to do large-scale developing, yet there are some fine Georgian streets, particularly South Mall, another waterway filled in as the city expanded.

There was a huge divide between rich and poor in the eighteenth century. Wealthy merchants lived luxurious lives, while poorer citizens barely scraped by. By the middle of the century there was appalling overcrowding, crime and poverty. Cork's first workhouse opened in 1747, and in the following decade Nano Nagle opened a school for the poor (this eventually became the religious order of the Presentation Sisters – to find out more about it, and the remarkable woman who founded it, you can visit Nano Nagle Place, a heritage centre on Abbey Street). Problems were exacerbated in the nineteenth century by the Great Famine of the 1840s, and in the twenty years that followed, it is estimated that over a quarter of a million people emigrated from Cork Harbour. The second half of the century, however, saw something of a recovery and much of the present city began to emerge, along with some of its finest architecture, including St Fin Barre's Cathedral, University College Cork, and a number of churches and religious buildings, such as St Vincent's in Sunday's Well. Many of the city's bridges also date from this time.

Irish nationalism was on the rise again towards the end of the nineteenth century and Cork was a base for the national Fenian movement. The city had always had a reputation for political rebelliousness. The 1916 Easter Rising took place mainly in Dublin, but its aftermath was felt all over the country, including Cork. Two successive lord mayors were martyred for the cause of Irish freedom: Tomás Mac Curtain was shot in front of his wife and child in 1920, while Terence MacSwiney, his successor, died on hunger strike in an English prison protesting the arrest of Ireland's democratically elected representatives. Things came to a head on the night of 11 December 1920, the infamous Burning of Cork, when parts of the city centre were set on fire by the Black and Tans (so called because of the colour of their uniforms). City Hall and much of the eastern side of St Patrick's Street were destroyed. A controversial treaty ended Ireland's War of Independence in 1921, but it partitioned the island and sparked off a bitter Civil War (1922–1923). Once this ended, things began to settle down, and the 1920s saw industry attracted to Cork, notably Ford and Dunlop. During the Second World War the city experienced an economic decline. However, the 1960s brought new investment, especially from chemical and engineering firms; Cork is still a centre for the pharmaceutical and engineering industries. The recession of the 1980s was followed by a boom in the 1990s – the Celtic Tiger – which ended in 2008. The country, and Cork, has been slowly recovering ever since.

Cork is now home to 120,000 people, and is the second largest city in Ireland. It is a pleasant place to stroll through, and has a fascinating history, which can be traced in its many beautiful buildings. The surrounding county is home to some of the most

Buskers, St Patrick's Street

spectacular landscape in Ireland, with a wild and rugged coastline as well as lush, green valleys dotted with country houses and castles (including Blarney Castle, where you can kiss the world-famous Blarney Stone). And the city is only a short distance from the charming seaside towns of Cobh and Kinsale (which have their own chapters in this book). All that remains now is for you to stroll around this relaxed and welcoming city while taking in the architectural treasures, but make sure you make the most of its thriving arts scene, shops, atmospheric pubs and world-class restaurants.

DID YOU KNOW?

One of the Lord Mayor of Cork's duties is to throw a dart into the River Lee at the entrance of the harbour, symbolically claiming jurisdiction over the waters. This ceremony dates back to 1500, when Henry VII granted the mayor jurisdiction over the harbour, and is still performed every three years.

Ulster Bank,
St Patrick's
Street

NOTE: THE WALKS

The walks in this book are arranged around Cork's different districts, such as the medieval city or the St Patrick's Street area. Each one starts where the previous one left off and there are eight in all, starting with Shandon in the north and working all the way around to Sunday's Well in the west. There is also a Further Afield section, which takes in buildings and places a little outside the city centre, such as the Lough and Blackrock Castle, as well as castles and country houses only a short distance from Cork and well worth a visit, like Fota House and Blarney Castle. There are also walks in Cobh and Kinsale, neighbouring seaside towns which have a shared history with the city. Finally, there is a chapter that explains the architectural styles mentioned in the book, as well as a glossary of architectural terms. The book ends with a listings section containing contact details for the attractions mentioned in it. All that remains is to wish you a pleasant time strolling around the beautiful city of Cork!

SHANDON

Approximate walking time: 1 hour 30 minutes

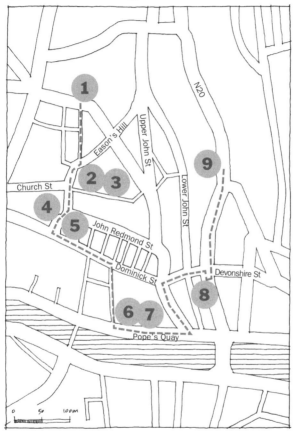

THE WALK: KEY

1 **St Mary and St Anne's Cathedral**

2 **St Anne's Shandon**

3 **Skiddy's Almshouse**

4 **Cork Butter Museum**

5 **Firkin Crane Theatre**

6 **St Mary's**

7 **Cork Civic Trust**

8 **Dominican Priory**

9 **Murphy Heineken Brewery**

W E BEGIN IN SHANDON, a hilly part of Cork with steep streets, some of them stepped, offering pretty views of the city below. Shandon is one of the best preserved parts of Cork, having escaped the floods and fires that periodically ravaged the city over the centuries. Its name comes from an old fort (*sean dún*) that used to be located here. It is also the most famous part of the city because of a song celebrating the bells of St Anne's Shandon, a charming church behind which lies Skiddy's Almshouse, a surprisingly intact early eighteenth-century poorhouse. A church dedicated to St Mary was built here in the Middle Ages but this was replaced by the lofty Cathedral of St Mary and St Anne in the nineteenth century. Close to this sit the imposing Cork Butter Museum and the Firkin Crane Theatre, while down on the River Lee sits the elegant St Mary's, and next door to it is the Cork Civic Trust. The walk also takes you via the Cork Arts Theatre and the Murphy Heineken Brewery.

1 St Mary and St Anne's Cathedral

This Catholic place of worship is also known as the North Cathedral and was intended as a statement of Catholic pride after years of discrimination in Ireland. Located in the hills north of the city, it gets its double name from the fact that it encompasses the ecclesiastical parish of St Mary and the civil parish of St Anne. Begun in 1799 on the site of an older chapel, it was completed by 1808. No one knows who the original architect was but after a fire that left the building little more than a shell in 1820, George Pain remodelled it in a light Gothic style. The central tower was added in 1862 by John Benson. Constructed of an attractive (and typically Cork) mix of red sandstone and grey limestone, it was intended to be even more impressive but the 60m (200-foot) spire was never added. The pinnacles on the tower's four corners do, however, ensure that it is 3m (10 feet) taller than the nearby St Anne's Shandon. Across the street from the cathedral's south entrance is an imposing **Presbytery**, a symmetrical, gabled four-storey Victorian Gothic house in red brick and limestone.

∙∙

DID YOU KNOW?

One of the vaults under an earlier incarnation of St Mary and St Anne's Cathedral was opened around 1780 and the body of Reverend McDaniel was found to be in an almost perfect state of preservation. News of this 'miracle' quickly spread throughout the city and crowds of people came to see the body. The crowds grew so large that an army sergeant was posted as guard. Unfortunately, curiosity got the better of him and he decided to poke the body with his cane, breaking off its nose. He was punished for this lack of respect and the body was promptly reburied. A century later a local historian had the vault reopened; the body was still in a near-perfect state of preservation, with its nose still missing.

2 St Anne's Shandon

Walk along Cathedral Street and turn right onto Chapel Street and you will see the tall tower of St Anne's Shandon ahead of you. Named after the mother of the Virgin Mary, this is one of Cork's most famous landmarks as well as one of the oldest churches still in use in the city. Built between 1722 and 1726, it occupies the site of St Mary's (which was destroyed during the Siege of Cork in 1690). A tax on coal coming into the city was levied to pay for the rebuilding of Protestant churches damaged or destroyed during the siege. The church is in a simple, understated Neoclassicism, and its tower is the main attraction. Known locally as the 'pepper pot', because its top three storeys taper inwards, it is 36m (120 feet) high and topped by a small dome under a weather vane in the form of a gilded salmon. (Thought to be a reference to Cork's fishing industry, it is more likely the Christian symbol based on Jesus having encouraged his early followers to be 'fishers of men'.) Unusually, the tower's south and west façades are grey limestone, while the east and north are red sandstone. There have been many theories for this, including weather protection, or that the different stones faced the landscape from which they came, or that they represented the colours of Cork's flag (which is red and white). The most likely explanation, however, comes from Crofton Croker, who thought the more expensive limestone façades were placed facing the areas where most of the church's parishioners and benefactors lived. The tower has wonderful views and is home to the famous bells which inspired the song 'The Bells of Shandon' by a homesick Fr Prout – the pen name of Fr Sylvester Mahony who spent most of his life in London. He died in Paris in 1866 but his remains were brought back to this churchyard. Each side of the tower also contains a clock face. Installed in 1847 and affectionately known as the 'four-faced liar', the hands on the east and west run slightly fast, especially in windy weather. This is probably because they are so very large (only Big Ben in London has larger clock faces).

St Anne's Shandon

DID YOU KNOW?

The clock on St Anne's Shandon was built for the benefit of poor people, to help ensure they took their medicines at the right time.

ST ANNE'S SHANDON
Opening times: Monday – Saturday, 10 a.m. – 4 p.m., Sunday, 11.30 a.m. – 4 p.m. (March to May and October); Monday – Saturday, 10 a.m. – 5 p.m., Sunday, 11.30 a.m. – 4.30 p.m. (June to September); Monday – Saturday, 11 a.m. – 3 p.m., Sunday, 11.30 a.m. – 3 p.m. (November to February)
Admission charges

3 Skiddy's Almshouse

Leave St Anne's Shandon and turn left onto the rather oddly named Bob and Joan's Walk. Then take the next left onto a small alleyway and Skiddy's Almshouse will be on your right. Founded as a charitable institution to look after elderly widows in 1620, it was the second almshouse funded by a wealthy Cork merchant called Stephen Skiddy (who had made his money in the London wine trade). It was unusual in that it was open to both Catholics and Protestants. This charming L-shaped building dates from 1718, making it one of the oldest in the city. The arched arcades were designed for the almshouse's elderly inhabitants to walk about while protected from the elements. Almost demolished in the 1960s, it fortunately survived and was restored in the 1970s by the Cork Preservation Society. Restored again in 2005, it won an award for the excellence of the work. The almshouse used to form part of a complex of charitable buildings behind St Mary's (the predecessor to St Anne's Shandon). This included a Green Coat Hospital and School which had statues of a boy and a girl on its gateposts –

Skiddy's Almshouse

hence the name Bob and Joan's Walk. The hospital and school were demolished in the 1950s, and all that was salvaged were the two statues, which were moved to St Anne's Shandon where they can still be seen in the bell tower.

SKIDDY'S ALMSHOUSE (GARDEN ONLY)
Opening times: Daily, 2 – 4 p.m.
Admission: free

4 Cork Butter Museum

Go back up Bob and Joan's Walk and turn left onto Exchange Street. The Cork Butter Museum will be on your right, with its main entrance in O'Connell Square, behind the large Neoclassical portico. This fascinating museum opened in 1997 and tells the story of Irish butter, with displays on the history of how it is made, a process that is thousands of years old. The Cork Butter Exchange began here as an outdoor market, on the grounds of the former Shandon Castle, in 1730. An indoor market was built in 1770, and it was here that butter was graded before being exported, not only to the United Kingdom (where it was the largest supplier of butter) but also to Europe, America and even the Caribbean. The exchange was extended by John Benson in 1849. His fine Neoclassical complex, with its magnificently scaled portico facing confidently down John Redmond Street, is centred on twin Roman Doric columns flanking the tall entrance archway which signals just how important the exchange was in the nineteenth century. By 1892 it was exporting half a million casks of butter annually; however, competition from other parts of Europe in the twentieth century led to it shutting down in 1924. The building became a hat factory before a fire shut that down in 1976. It was then revived as the **Shandon Craft Centre** in the 1980s and is a popular venue for local craftspeople

Cork Butter Museum

to display and sell their handcrafted wares. You can find everything from weavers to crystal cutters at work here. The centre is also a venue for free concerts in the summer.

CORK BUTTER MUSEUM
Opening times: Daily, 10 a.m.– 5 p.m. (March to October); Saturday and Sunday (only), 11 a.m. – 3 p.m. (November to February)
Admission charges

SHANDON CRAFT CENTRE
Opening times: Daily, 10 a.m.– 5 p.m. (March to October); Saturday and Sunday (only), 11 a.m. – 3 p.m. (November to February)
Admission charges

5 Firkin Crane Theatre

Facing the Cork Butter Museum across O'Connell Square is the Firkin Crane Theatre, a simple Neoclassical rotunda with a steep slate roof. This building was constructed in 1855 as a place for coopers (barrel-makers) to make or repair butter barrels, or firkins. Made out of American oak, these were used by the exchange across the square for the export of butter to the United Kingdom, Europe and North and Central America. The building was all but destroyed by a fire in the 1970s but was restored a decade later and is now a dance and cultural centre. It sits on the site of **Shandon Castle**, which was built in the late twelfth century by the Barrymores (who later built Fota House). Home to mayors and governors of Cork, the castle was also a courthouse and jail where political prisoners were kept. Once dominating the city, it was destroyed during the Siege of Cork in 1690.

DID YOU KNOW?

Stones from the ruins of Shandon Castle were used for the building of St Anne's Shandon.

6 St Mary's

Ferry Lane

Go behind the Firkin Crane Theatre and turn left onto Dominick Street. Take the second right down Waggett's Lane, which turns into Ferry Lane, a stepped and gated street that leads out onto Pope's Quay, which was named after a wealthy widow who built it in 1718. St Mary's will be on your left overlooking the river. This exquisite essay in Grecian simplicity has to rank as one of the finest Neoclassical buildings in the city. Dominicans have had a presence in Cork since the thirteenth century, when they built a church called St Mary's of the Isle on what is now Sharman Crawford Street. Then in 1784, decades before Catholic Emancipation in 1829, they built a house and chapel on Dominick Street. After Emancipation they felt bold enough to commission a grand new church, one of the first Catholic places of worship built in the city after Emancipation. It was designed by local architect Kearns Deane who waived his fee (a generous act for the Protestant architect of a Catholic church). The original design had tall towers on either end of the façade but these were never built. The

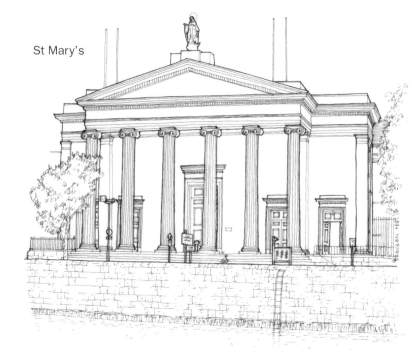

St Mary's

foundation stone was laid in 1832 and the church opened for worship seven years later, an event celebrated by a grand banquet attended by the Liberator, Daniel O'Connell, himself. Kearns Deane died of TB in 1847 so it was his older brother, Sir Thomas Deane, who supervised the building of the fluted Ionic hexastyle portico, which makes the building such a landmark, especially when seen reflected in the River Lee.

• •

DID YOU KNOW?

Ferry Lane takes its name from a ferry that used to operate between here and Lavitt's Quay in the seventeenth century.

7 Cork Civic Trust

Next door to St Mary's stands the Cork Civic Trust, a voluntary non-profit organisation aimed at preserving and enhancing the civic and architectural heritage of Cork city and county. Housed in an elegant and understated Queen Anne townhouse dating from the beginning of the eighteenth century, this three-storey, red-brick mansion has five bays symmetrically arranged around a delicately carved doorway which features a finely carved broken pediment with scrolls. One of the oldest surviving houses in the city, it is also considered one of the finest. Thought to have been built for Lord Burlington, the early eighteenth-century arbiter of taste in architecture, it is unlikely that he ever lived here. (Richard Boyle was not only the third Earl of Burlington, he was also the fourth Earl of Cork, hence his connection to the city.) In the nineteenth century the house became home to wealthy butter merchant Henry Maultby, whose cooperage (barrel-making factory) supplied Cork's many breweries as well as the Cork Butter Exchange. For a brief time in the late nineteenth century it was The County and City of

Cork Civic Trust

THE EARLS OF CORK

Richard Boyle, an Anglo-Irish politician from Canterbury in England, was made Earl of Cork in 1620. He had married a wealthy Irish heiress and bought large estates in County Cork. Remarkably, four of his sons went on to be awarded titles of their own. However, the one who did not is probably the most famous: Robert Boyle was a scientist, and Boyle's Law is named after him. The fourth Earl of Cork is better known by one of his other titles, Lord Burlington. He was a gifted amateur architect and designed Chiswick House in London for himself (with the aid of William Kent). He was the arbiter of all things tasteful in early eighteenth-century London but as he had no sons the Burlington title died out (the Cork title passed to a distant cousin and there is still an Earl of Cork, the fifteenth). Burlington's daughter married the fourth Duke of Devonshire (bringing the family Lismore Castle as part of her dowry). The second in line to the dukedom is still traditionally known as the Earl of Burlington.

Cork Hospital for Women and Children but by 1901 was a residence once again, although broken up into smaller lodgings – and it was falling into disrepair. By the 1980s it was very dilapidated and was taken over by Cork City Council. It then spent a short time as home to a theatre company before being turned into the Cork Civic Trust in the 1990s. Next door to the Trust stands the **Dominican Centre**, a jaunty single-storey Art Deco building that turns the sharp corner onto Mulgrave Road smoothly. Originally Daly's Butter Merchants, it was one of many such merchants located in this part of the city so as to be close to the Cork Butter Exchange.

8 Dominican Priory

Walk up the steeply sloping Mulgrave Road and turn left onto Dominic Street. The **Dominican Priory** will be on your left. This large complex of religious buildings was built by William Atkins in the 1850s. Previously the Dominicans had occupied a house on Dominic Street and also some of the land on which part of the Cork Butter Museum now stands. They sold both plots to allow the Butter Exchange to extend in 1849, and chose to develop this land at the corner of Dominic Street and Mulgrave Road instead. This fine three-storey Italianate structure is constructed of a reddish-brown sandstone with light grey limestone dressing. Thought to be a

Gateway, Dominican Priory

remodelling of an earlier Georgian house, its architect seems to have had difficulty in deciding whether he wanted a Neoclassical or a Gothic design; the resulting compromise, with its arched windows, gives it an almost Romanesque feel: solid yet attractive. The attractiveness is much enhanced by its six-storey bell tower which features windows that get larger as each floor ascends. This is a charming building, well situated on its sloping site, and making a pretty prospect from the other side of the River Lee (from where the bell tower of St Anne's Shandon can be seen nestling behind it). Return to Mulgrave Street and cross it, taking the stairs down to Devonshire Street, then take the second right onto Carroll's Quay and the **Cork Arts Theatre** will be on your right. Located on the ground floor of a large residential block, it was founded in 1976. The 'CAT Club', as it is affectionately known, quickly established itself as a valuable

Dominican Priory with
St Anne's Shandon

platform for home-grown talent to start theatrical careers and is an important hub for networking in the Cork arts scene. The theatre was refurbished in 2006 and provides an interesting programme of events throughout the year. The Cork Repertory Company was founded here in 2012.

DID YOU KNOW?

When Oliver Cromwell was running short of artillery during his Irish campaigns in the 1640s he melted down the bells from Catholic churches, turning them into cannon. When someone protested about this he said that since gunpowder had been invented by a priest, it was appropriate that he promote bells into cannons.

9 Murphy Heineken Brewery

Leave the Cork Arts Theatre by turning left up Carroll's Quay. Follow this wide and meandering road until you come to the Murphy Heineken Brewery on your left. Originally founded as

Murphy's Brewery in 1856, it was better known as the Lady's Well Brewery (until 1983, when it was purchased by Heineken). The last major porter brewery established in Cork, Murphy's stout was popular, rapidly eclipsing older rival Beamish and Crawford to become the largest brewery in the city and, by 1906, the second-largest in the country (after Guinness). Murphy's made clever use of advertising (something later copied by Guinness). In 1891 they hired Eugene Sandow, World Weightlifting Champion, to endorse their product; the image of the strongman lifting a horse became the company's trademark. The last heir to the Murphy business died in 1980, by which time the company was in bad shape. It was saved from closure by Heineken (who, ironically, later closed down the rival Beamish and Crawford in 2009). Established in the grounds of what had been Cork's **Foundling Hospital**, an organisation founded in 1147 to look after babies found abandoned in the city, the complex is a large one and was once dominated by a 60m (200-foot) chimney. Demolished in 1985 because of structural concerns, all the buildings on the east side of Leitrim Street were also demolished, including craftsmen's shops and stables. Fortunately, the robust Victorian malthouse (designed by T. Hynes in 1889) still stands. Five storeys of roughly finished sandstone dressed with limestone, there is a three-bay malting kiln at the southern end and a tower to the north, both of which have pyramidal roofs. Steel-and-glass extensions were added when the building was converted into offices in 1992.

Link to the MacCurtain Street to City Hall walk:
Leave the Murphy Heineken Brewery and retrace your steps down Carroll's Quay before taking the first left onto Leitrim Street, which will lead you to Coburg Street, where you should also turn left and you will come to MacCurtain Street.

Shandon

MACCURTAIN STREET TO CITY HALL

Approximate walking time: 2 hours and 30 minutes

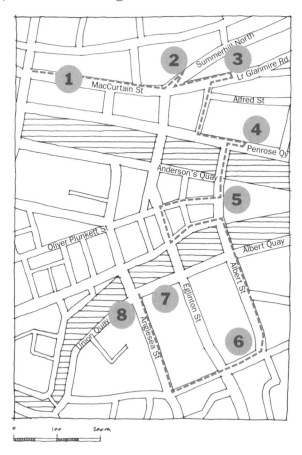

THE WALK: KEY

1 **MacCurtain Street**
2 **Trinity Presbyterian Church**
3 **St Patrick's**
4 **Penrose Quay**

5 **Custom House**
6 **The Elysian**
7 **City Hall**
8 **Union Quay**

T HIS PART OF THE CITY is known for its pubs and restaurants, especially MacCurtain Street, which is where you will also find the Everyman Theatre. This street contains some of the city's best examples of Victorian commercial architecture, while at its east end there are two of Cork's finest churches: the Gothic Trinity Presbyterian Church and the Neoclassical St Patrick's. This walk also takes you through places that are a testament to Cork's rich maritime history, including Penrose Quay and the Custom House. It takes in two of the city's most iconic architectural landmarks: The Elysian, a recently built and very tall residential tower, and City Hall, which presides majestically over the southern channel of the River Lee. Finally, you can visit some of the lively pubs on Union Quay.

1 MacCurtain Street

At the beginning of MacCurtain Street you will see **Patrick's Hill** to your left, a steeply sloped Georgian residential street that leads down from a place known as 'the ridge', and has wonderful views

Patrick's Hill

of the city. This street runs all the way down to the river at St Patrick's Bridge. **MacCurtain Street** was originally called King Street and was renamed in honour of Tomás Mac Curtain, an Irish freedom fighter who was passionate about Irish culture, music and language. He was secretary of the Gaelic League and a founding member of the Irish Volunteers. He became Lord Mayor of Cork in January of 1920, but was shot by members of the Royal Irish Constabulary (RIC) just two months later. The murder was met with outrage, not least because it was carried out in front of his wife and son. His funeral was one of the largest ever seen in Cork. (By a strange coincidence, the members of the RIC who committed the crime were actually stationed in this street.) On your right-hand side you will see the wrought-iron and glass entrance portico to the **Everyman Theatre**. Officially called the Everyman Palace

Everyman
Theatre

Theatre, it is a popular venue, with a beautifully restored Victorian interior. It began life in 1897 as a music hall called the Palace of Varieties. It then turned into a cinema in 1930. Now once again a theatre, it has a capacity of 630 and hosts a varied programme, from theatre to music. Across the street is the **Cork Baptist Church**, a jauntily asymmetrical building railed off from the street. Built in 1892, this light Gothic place of worship is built in a warm (almost orange-coloured) red brick with limestone trimmings. It has a short gabled tower and elaborate carving over the door, featuring a quotation from the Bible. Twinned point-arched windows sit under a bullseye window topped by a small limestone belfry missing its bell. Further down, on the same side of the street, sits the magnificent **Hibernia Buildings**, one of the finest Victorian commercial buildings in the city. Originally designed by Robert Walker in 1879, it was later altered (and actually improved) by Arthur Hill. The central block has a central gable which seems too small for its façade (the original design). Hill added the two-storey oriel windows sitting on wide engaged columns over the arches flanking the central block, and linking this block to the three-bay gabled side buildings. Hill also altered the central block's windows, much improving Walker's original design. It is a lovely example of Victorian Romanesque, with round-arched windows and foliate capitals on the columns. Now home to shops and a hotel.

Further down the street on your right is the **Metropole Hotel**. Known locally as the Met, it opened in 1897 and was also designed by Arthur Hill. Edward VII is reputed to have had tea here when he visited Cork for the Great Exhibition in 1903. It is a busy Victorian Gothic building, with bay windows, recessed arches, pointed dormer windows, and a delightful corner turret overlooking the junction

DID YOU KNOW?

The name 'Hadji' denotes a Muslim who has made the pilgrimage to Mecca.

with Harley's Street. It was one of Cork's most glamorous hotels in the 1950s and 1960s, and hosted Hollywood stars. It fell on hard times in the 1970s before eventually being refurbished. It reopened in 2001. The hotel's street front used to be shops, one of which was the **Hadji Bey et Cie** sweet shop, which specialised in Turkish Delight. The man who founded it, Harutan Batmazian, came to Cork from Armenia in 1903 to set up a sweet stall at the Great Exhibition. When the exhibition ended he then set up shop at the Metropole, and quickly became a Cork institution. After his retirement the business went into decline and closed in the 1980s. Sultan Delight has opened further up the street, on the same side as the Metropole, where it is once again possible to buy the beautifully wrapped and delicious sweets. Continue along MacCurtain Street and you will come to **Thompson House** on the corner of York Street on your left. Originally Thompson's Bakery (you can still see the sign for Thompson and Son over the arched doorway), this warehouse-like

Metropole Hotel

Victorian commercial building consists of two five-storey gabled blocks (the right-hand one with a truncated tower) linked by a smaller three-storey central block. Designed by Robert Walker in 1889, it is the most relaxed of the Victorian commercial buildings on MacCurtain Street. It has round-arched windows in a red-brick façade with limestone dressing. The low tower was added in 1914. It is now home to **Tigh Filí**, a multi-purpose arts centre with a brightly lit gallery space showcasing local artists' work. There are also performance spaces, artists' studios and an atmospheric café.

••

DID YOU KNOW?

British film star Dawn Adams came to Cork to attend the Film Festival in the 1950s and scandalised the management of the Metropole Hotel when she ordered her bath to be filled with milk. The hotel refused, on the grounds that it was too extravagant in a city where people were finding it hard to make ends meet, but the story made headlines around the world.

2 Trinity Presbyterian Church

Continue down MacCurtain Street and you will come to **Summerhill North** on your left. This is where many of Cork's wealthier citizens moved in the nineteenth century. They could afford the horses and carriages needed to get here. It became more accessible once bridges began to be built over the river. Overlooking this junction is the former **Carmichael School**, a delightful essay in Gothic-revival architecture (see the Architectural Styles chapter for an illustration). Named after a prominent local benefactor, this pretty little limestone building has a squat bell tower and is in good condition despite its current lack of use. Sitting on top of the hill overlooking the former school is **Trinity Presbyterian Church**, a beautifully restrained Gothic Revival church dating from 1861. The spire soars 42m (140 feet) into the air and leans a little at the top. Designed by English architect J. Tarring, it is constructed in a lovely light-grey limestone and is the only example in the city of Kentish ragstone, a hard grey limestone from Kent in the UK. The plan is cruciform, with shallow transepts, and large buttresses framing the leaded-glass windows which contain delicate carved-stone tracery. Presbyterians have been in Cork since 1675; they first had a Meeting House on Watergate Lane (now Hanover Street). They then built what was known as the Scots Church on Queen Street in the 1840s but soon found it too small and decided to build this church instead, on the more spacious Summerhill North site. They chose the name Trinity because they were Trinitarian (i.e. they believe in the doctrine of the Trinity, as opposed to Unitarians, who do not).

••

DID YOU KNOW?

The kink in the spire of Trinity Presbyterian Church is said to have been made deliberately by disgruntled workers in a wage dispute. Although a nice (or perhaps not such a nice) story, it is probably simply the result of bad workmanship; a pity on such a beautiful building.

3 St Patrick's

Retrace your steps down Summerhill North and turn left at the sharp corner onto Lower Glanmire Road. This is known as **Coliseum Corner**, named after the Coliseum Cinema, which operated here from 1913 to 1964. On your left, a little up the street, you will see the impressive Neoclassical façade of St Patrick's. Designed by George Pain, it was built between 1832 and 1836. The pedimented Corinthian hexastyle portico sits on a high base and is

St Patrick's

surmounted by a cruciform tempietto upholding a rotunda encircled by figures of saints. The limestone façades have giant pilasters. The interior is still intact, including pews, floor covering and chancel decoration. Unusually, for such a strict Greek Revival building, the church doors do not align with the spaces between the portico columns (probably because the portico was built so much later than the rest of the church). A number of famous Cork writers are associated with St Patrick's, including Fr Francis Sylvester Mahony (better known as Fr Prout, author of 'The Bells of Shandon'), and short-story writer Frank O'Connor (real name Michael O'Donovan). 'First Confession' is a story about a young boy called Jackie being dragged to his First Confession by a tyrannical older sister, Nora.

• •

DID YOU KNOW?

A magnificent silver chalice made for the Franciscans in 1648 was generously donated to St Patrick's in 1859 by a Mrs Simms in memory of her husband, John. No one is sure what happened to it in the intervening years, but the chalice then appeared for auction in Kilkenny in the 1990s, with a hefty reserve. The auctioneers refused to give any information about the seller (or how they came to be in possession of it), but when it did not attract a buyer, representatives of St Patrick's managed to buy it back (and for considerably less than the reserve). It can now be seen in its rightful home.

4 Penrose Quay

Return down Lower Glanmire Road and turn left onto Ship Street, then take a left at the river along Penrose Quay and you will come to **Penrose House** at the end of the block, at the corner of Railway Street. This used to be the Steampacket Office, a shipping company founded in the 1820s as the St George Steam Packet Company (hence the statue of St George battling the dragon over the pediment). The company moved here in 1831. A well-proportioned Neoclassical building, it has an elegant portico of four Ionic columns under a pediment and is thought possibly to have been designed by the Pain brothers. There have been some cosmetic

Penrose House

changes to the façade over the years, including the addition of a coarse frieze, and a boxy bay window to the right of the entrance. Penrose Quay was also the location of the terminus of the Great Southern and Western railway line. This fine Gothic station building was demolished once Kent Station was built nearby in the 1890s.

5 Custom House

Walk back up Penrose Quay and turn left across Michael Collins Bridge and you will see the Custom House on your left, occupying this prominent site at the tip of Cork's city-centre island. This is where the two channels of the River Lee, separated far to the west, join together again as the river flows into Cork Harbour. The rather staid Neoclassical Custom House is constructed of limestone and has an unpretentious, businesslike façade appropriate to its function. Designed by Abraham Hargrave, it dates from 1814 and if you look at the centrally placed pediment you can see a carving of Cork's coat of arms, which has the motto '*Statio bene fida carinis*' ('a safe harbour for ships'). Cork has one of the world's finest natural harbours, and the buildings here are a reminder of the city's rich maritime history. It was from here that the butter and other products were exported that made the city's merchants so rich. The Custom House complex is large, deceptively so. It forms a long isosceles triangle sticking well into the harbour, which is belied by the relatively narrow frontage of the Custom House and its flanking walls. The complex includes a harbour commissioner's office and rows and rows of bonded warehouses. The port grew increasingly busy throughout the nineteenth century, which encouraged labourers to migrate to the city, greatly increasing its population. Facing the Custom House is Oliver Plunkett Street, home to two of the city's most famous **newspapers**. The *Irish Examiner* was founded as the *Cork Examiner* by Francis Maguire in 1841; the *Evening Echo* was also founded here, in 1892, and is still going strong.

DID YOU KNOW?

Cork is credited with being the first city in Ireland or Great Britain to print a newspaper. Oliver Cromwell was accompanied by a printer on his Irish campaigns and set up *The Corke Mercury* in 1649 for propaganda purposes. This first 'newspaper' may have resembled a modern-day broadsheet but it mainly contained military dispatches.

6 The Elysian

Continue along Oliver Plunkett Street Lower and turn left onto Clontarf Street, then take a left onto **Lapp's Quay**. One of Cork's great attractions is that the city is built on an island in a river, and its waterfronts have always been busy – and sport a variety of architectural styles, from warehouses to gracious Georgian homes, as well as numerous Neoclassical and Gothic churches. The quays are no longer so busy commercially but some parts of them have been attractively redeveloped into pleasant places to go out. This part of Lapp's Quay has been entirely redeveloped, with offices, hotels, bars and cafés overlooking the river. There is also a wide boardwalk projecting out over the water, with seats, and a little jetty down on the water, for those who want to arrive by boat. Continue along Lapp's Quay, then turn right over Éamon de Valera Bridge and go down Albert Street (which was named in honour of Queen Victoria's German-born husband, Prince Albert) and you will see the red-painted **National Sculpture Factory** on your left after the junction with Albert Road. Jointly funded by the Arts Council of Ireland and Cork City Council, this is an organisation that provides support to artists through residencies, lecture programmes, cultural exchanges, masterclasses and professional-development work-shops. It also helps them to promote their work. Housed in the old Albert Street Station, originally a terminus of the Cork, Blackrock and Passage Railway, this simple building was designed by John Benson in 1873. Continue along Albert Street, which will turn to the right, and you will come to **The Elysian** at the corner of Eglinton Street. This is a mixed-use

The Elysian

development dating from the first decade of the twenty-first century – the era of the Celtic Tiger economic boom. Occupying a large site, it consists of a number of interconnected blocks, most of which are six to eight storeys in height. There is also a massive seventeen-storey residential tower whose apartments command wonderful views of the city. The tower is 68m (224 feet) tall, making it the tallest building in the country – The Spire in Dublin is taller, at 120 m (393 feet), but that is not a building.

NATIONAL SCULPTURE FACTORY
Opening times: Varies, check website
Admission: free

• •

DID YOU KNOW?

The Elysian is the tallest building in the Republic of Ireland.

Continue along Albert Street, past the junction with Eglinton Road, and you will be on Old Station Road. Turn right onto Anglesea Street and you will see a **Garda Station** on the corner to your right. This symmetrical four-storey block is in the Postmodern style. The ground floor is rusticated ashlar, while the rest of the building is rendered in a robust roughcast. The façade sprouts a variety of flourishes, including balconies and bay windows that support projecting upper floors. It looks a little like the sort of apartment complex built for East European Communist leaders for their holidays. Next door to the Garda Station is a **Fire Station**, a no-nonsense five-storey Modernist building. Facing these two buildings is a much better essay in urban architecture. This enormous complex of the former **Model School** is a delight. A busy red-brick complex stepped back from the street and regarded as one of the finest model schools ever built in Ireland, it was designed by E.T. Owen and R.A. Gibbons around 1862 (with some later additions by James McMullen). It is nicely proportioned, with red-brick façades enlivened by polychromatic brickwork and zigzag ornamentation around the windows. This rambling complex is given a nice focus by its asymmetrically placed bell tower. The whole place has been converted into a courthouse complex.

Continue along Anglesea Street and you will see **City Hall** on your right. This elegant building is home to Cork City Council's administrative headquarters and was opened in 1936. Designed by Alfred Jones and Stephen Kelly, it was built by the local firm of Sisk and Company and constructed in a lightly glistening limestone. The old City Hall was destroyed by fire on the night of 11 December 1920. This was during Ireland's War of Independence, when the Black and Tans went on a rampage, an event immortalised as the Burning of Cork (for more on this see the St Patrick's Street and Environs walk). This symmetrical three-storey building is in a stripped-down Neoclassical style, with three limestone façades,

City Hall

each with a breakfront. The main façade has paired Roman Doric columns in antis, meaning they are free-standing in front of an arcaded porch, and stand under a full entablature surmounted by a copper-domed clock tower. A major new extension was added in 2007 in a gorgeously handled Modernism – all glass and white stone, and an elegant counterpoint to the main building, which it makes no attempt to imitate (quite rightly). This was one of the last large-scale Neoclassical stone buildings ever built in Ireland, and its riverside location considerably adds to its urban presence; it almost seems to act as a gateway to the east of the city. The fact that the building is still in use, and for its original purpose, also adds greatly to its charm.

••

DID YOU KNOW?

The British government footed the bill for building Cork's new City Hall as a gesture of reconciliation for what had happened to the old one.

8 Union Quay

On the other side of Anglesea Street is Union Quay. Formerly known as Allen's Marsh, it was renamed to commemorate the passing of the Act of Union between Britain and Ireland in 1801. This part of the city was devastated on the night of 11 December 1920, the night known as the Burning of Cork. There used to be a red-brick Royal Irish Constabulary (RIC) barracks here dating

from 1876. It survived the conflagration of 1920 only to be destroyed by anti-Treaty forces during the Civil War. It was rebuilt in the 1920s but has not survived to the present day. What does survive, however, is the tradition of the 'early house' pubs: these are places with a special licence to open early to cater to dock workers and other labourers who have to start early. One of the best-known early houses in Cork is **Charlie's**, busy morning, noon and night. It is also a popular place to catch live performances of traditional Irish music.

Charlie's, Union Quay

Link to South Mall and Oliver Plunkett Street walk:
Cross Parnell Bridge.

SOUTH MALL AND OLIVER PLUNKETT STREET

Approximate walking time: 1 hour and 30 minutes

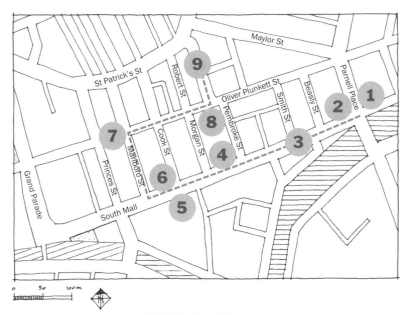

THE WALK: KEY

1 **Cork Savings Bank**

2 **Provincial Bank (former)**

3 **South Mall**

4 **Imperial Hotel**

5 **Assembly Rooms**

6 **AIB**

7 **Oliver Plunkett Street**

8 **GPO**

9 **Winthrop Street**

L IKE A NUMBER of other major thoroughfares in Cork's city centre, South Mall was once a waterway. Built as a gracious residential street, it runs west from Parnell Place to Grand Parade and is the heart of the city's financial and banking sector – this is also where you will find the architectural gems of the Cork Savings Bank, the former Provincial Bank and AIB. The street is also home to the Imperial Hotel, which began life as the Commercial Rooms. The Assembly Rooms add a dash of Victorian colour to an otherwise sedate Georgian streetscape. This walk takes you up Oliver Plunkett Street, a lively shopping street parallel to South Mall and home to the GPO as well as a number of restaurants. Finally, you will come out onto Winthrop Street, which is full of cafés with terraces and is a great place to take a break.

1 Cork Savings Bank

The competition to design this imposing Neoclassical building was won by brothers Thomas and Kearns Deane in 1839 and completed three years later. Thomas Deane had actually been architect of the

Cork Savings Bank

bank's original premises and had been made a trustee, a position he resigned when he won the competition. Facing City Hall across Parnell Bridge, this building's beautifully balanced façades elegantly address both Lapp's Quay and Parnell Place, each one a model of self-contained restraint, and both working well together when seen from a distance. The ground floor's horizontal coursing forms a carefully composed plinth from which the upper floor's pilasters and fluted Ionic engaged columns rise to support a simple entablature, into which the bank's name is incised in gold, a subtle contrast to the building's silvery limestone. The banking hall formerly contained a sculpture of William Crawford (by John Hogan from 1840), which is now housed in the Crawford Art Gallery (see the St Patrick's Street and Environs walk).

2 Provincial Bank (former)

Facing the Cork Savings Bank across Parnell Place is the former Provincial Bank at number 97 South Mall. Built in 1865, it replaced an earlier building dating from 1825. When seen in conjunction with the Cork Savings Bank across the street, these two Victorian masterpieces act like gateposts into Parnell Place (a much less architecturally distinguished street). Very different in style, they are actually quite similar in massing. Both are very well handled. Number 97's decoration is more exuberant than its restrained neighbour. The fact that it

Provincial Bank
(former)

is constructed of a duller grey limestone detracts, to a certain extent, from its appearance. Having said that, it is actually a very fine building. Designed by William G. Murray (who recycled an unsuccessful entry for the City Hall competition), this opulent Italian-style palazzo has arched windows set into its rusticated ground floor. The tall upper storey has Corinthian columns with capitals seemingly strung together by the carved swags and garlands that hang under the blind attic. The centre of this main floor has a three-bay projection under a pedimented portico, while the coats of arms of Irish towns are carved into the arches above the main windows.

3 South Mall

South Mall is built on reclaimed marshland. Dunscombe's Marsh was located on one of the islands lying to the east of the medieval walled city of Cork. As the city began to expand in the eighteenth century, these marshes were reclaimed and the waterways between them covered, so that by about 1800 the street layout we see today was in place. South Mall is one of Cork's most gracious (and intact) Georgian streets, the place where upper-middle class professionals lived. (It also had a northern counterpart called North Mall on the north bank

Georgian house, South Mall

of the River Lee which was equally fashionable – see the Medieval City walk.) Mostly Protestant, these people were the backbone of the city's professional and commercial life. The street has always been the professional heart of the city, and this tradition continues today, with many of the Georgian houses now home to some of Cork's most prestigious banks, law firms and stockbrokers.

4 Imperial Hotel

Continue along South Mall and you will come to the Imperial Hotel on your right after Pembroke Street. Originally built as Commercial Buildings in 1813, architect Thomas Deane was asked to design a series of meeting rooms for the Committee of Cork Merchants, and three years later these were expanded into a new premises along Pembroke Street to include a hotel and coach yard. The hotel's first guests began to stay in 1816, and there have been many prominent people here ever since, including writers, artists, musicians and politicians. Maureen O'Hara, Sir Walter Scott and Daniel O'Connell all stayed here. Charles Dickens gave a reading in the Clarence Room, and Franz Liszt held a piano recital here. It is also where Victorian travel writer William Thackeray met the Apostle of Temperance, Fr Theobald Mathew for tea (what else?). Commercial Buildings continued in its original function until 1948, when it was finally incorporated into the rest of the hotel. Later in the twentieth century, despite its glittering history (or perhaps because there was so very much of it) the hotel began to look somewhat faded but was brought back to its former glory by the Flynn family, who bought it in 1998 and thoroughly renovated it before reopening in 2006. Thankfully, the external character of the building has not changed much since Thomas Deane first designed it over two centuries ago.

· ·

DID YOU KNOW?

Irish revolutionary hero Michael Collins spent the last night of his life at the Imperial Hotel (in room 115). He was murdered in an ambush on 22 August 1922 while making his way back from west Cork.

5 Assembly Rooms

Further down South Mall, on your left, opposite the entrance to Cook Street, sit the Assembly Rooms. Designed by Richard Rolt Brash in 1860, this is an unusual dash of Victorian colour in an otherwise sombre street of Georgian houses and grand Neoclassical banks. Originally known as the Protestant Hall, it hosted a variety of entertainments, from popular lectures to opera performances. It turned into a cinema in 1911 (it was known as 'The Assems') but this ended in 1964 and it has been looking for a meaningful new function ever since. Fortunately, it is still in good condition. It has an elaborate façade and each floor has two decorated arches linked by bands of limestone. The stone bands are carved with foliage, as are the capitals on the polished marble engaged columns that support the arches. The façade's yellow brick contrasts nicely with its stonework. The words 'Assembly Rooms' are spelled out in cast-iron capital letters under the decorative balustrade, while busy-looking wrought-iron fanlights top out the ground-floor arches. It is a lovely building crying out for a new and imaginative use.

Assembly
Rooms

6 AIB

Facing the Assembly Rooms across South Mall, at the corner of Cook Street, sits the regional headquarters of Allied Irish Banks (AIB). Originally the Munster and Leinster Bank, it was established in 1885 when the Munster Bank was in danger of collapsing and had to be rescued (by local brewer James Murphy). It took on a new name to go with its fresh start. Later on, it amalgamated with a number of other Irish banks to form AIB. This imposing nine-bay, four-storey structure was built by local firm Sisk and Company in 1914 and is in a lovely silvery limestone which fits seamlessly into the streetscape. Giant fluted Ionic engaged columns rise from a rusticated base topped by an entablature supporting balustrades masking the top floor's attic. The end pavilions sport the names 'Munster' and 'Leinster', over which can be seen the provinces' coats of arms: three crowns, and a harp, respectively.

7 Oliver Plunkett Street

Continue along South Mall and turn right up Marlboro Street, then turn right onto Oliver Plunkett Street, one of the city's main shopping streets. Home to a wide variety of architectural styles, they all seem to fit snugly together, probably because there is just so much buzz on the street itself. Originally laid out in the eighteenth century in the area known as Dunscombe's Marsh, initially it was called George's Street in honour of George I but when Ireland became independent in 1922 it was renamed after a seventeenth-century martyr and Archbishop of Armagh. It is a narrower street than some of its neighbours (like South Mall, Grand Parade or St Patrick's Street) but this is what gives it its special charm (it won an award for being a Great Street in 2016). Always bustling, it is home to a wide variety of bars, cafés and restaurants, and is also one of the most popular places to shop in the city (probably because its shops are not quite so expensive as some of its more upmarket neighbours).

DR JAMES BARRY, FEMALE SURGEON

Dr James Miranda Steuart Barry was born Margaret Ann Bulkley in a house on Oliver Plunkett Street around 1789 (when it was called George's Street). In 1809, with the aid of her mother, she enrolled at the University of Edinburgh Medical School but because women were not allowed to study medicine at that time, Margaret pretended to be a man, taking the name James Barry. After graduating in 1812, Dr Barry enlisted in the British army and by 1816 had risen to the rank of assistant surgeon at the Cape Colony garrison in South Africa. By the time she retired, Dr Barry was inspector general of military hospitals, the second highest medical office in the British army. Barry not only improved conditions for wounded soldiers, but also for natives. She performed the first successful caesarean operation in South Africa, despite her only knowledge of it being from a book (the child, a boy, was named James Barry Munnik in her honour). Suspicions as to Dr Barry's gender were usually squashed when confronted by her famously bad temper. This temper, coupled with rumours of a 'homosexual' relationship with Lord Somerset, forced Barry back to Britain in 1828. She then went on to serve in Mauritius, Trinidad and St Helena, but her bad temper always got her into trouble. It was only after her death in 1865 that it was discovered she was a woman. The army sealed her records for a century. Dr Barry is buried in Kensal Rise cemetery, London, with her name and rank engraved on the headstone.

DID YOU KNOW?

Although Dr Barry was famously bad-tempered, she was not without humour. Once, when a clergyman sent her a note requesting she extract a tooth, she sent him a blacksmith instead, with a tongs.

8 GPO

Continue up Oliver Plunkett Street and you will come to the General Post Office (GPO) on your right at the corner of Pembroke Street. Just in front of the GPO stands a row of four buildings. These are interesting, not so much for their architecture, which is unremarkable, but for the fact that they are the oldest buildings on the street, dating from the 1720s. The GPO is a large limestone structure that curves its way around onto Pembroke Street. It began life as the George's Theatre in 1760 (named after the original street name). It then suffered a bad fire in

GPO

1840 but managed to reopen shortly afterwards, changing its name to the Theatre Royal. This incarnation was designed by architect John Benson. Sadly, fire struck again thirteen years later and the theatre closed down for good. Eventually the building was sold to the Irish Postal Service in 1875 and reopened as the GPO in 1877. J.H. Owen was responsible for its new design, which incorporated some of Benson's old theatre (you can still see some of the original red sandstone on the upper floors on the Oliver Plunkett Street side). This was further extended around 1905 by T.J. Mellon, an architect from the Office of Public Works. Neither seems to have been particularly inspired with their designs here: the building is large but pedestrian, and seems oddly unassertive for such a prominent corner.

• •

DID YOU KNOW?

The shouts of 'Echo' can still be heard today by the *Evening Echo* newspaper seller outside the GPO's main entrance. This harks back to a time when the post office was a bustling hub of activity serving the city as its main telegraph and telephone exchange.

9 Winthrop Street

Tucked away upstairs at number 108 Oliver Plunkett Street (on the corner of Winthrop Street) is the **Hi-B Bar**. This is something of a Cork institution and feels more like someone's sitting room than a pub. The piano in the corner is put to good use by punters and there is an impressive collection of (mostly classical) music behind the bar. Around the corner on Winthrop Street is **The Long Valley**, another popular local institution and steeped in Cork's history and literary tradition. Winthrop Street itself, which faces the GPO, is a busy little thoroughfare that links Oliver Plunkett Street to St

Patrick's Street and is a wonderful place to stop for a coffee, drink or bite to eat. There are plenty of places to choose from, and many of the cafés and bars have terraces overlooking the street, making it the perfect place to watch the world go by or listen to the buskers who ply their trade here.

Winthrop Street

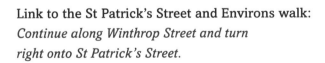

Link to the St Patrick's Street and Environs walk:
Continue along Winthrop Street and turn right onto St Patrick's Street.

South Mall and Oliver Plunkett Street

ST PATRICK'S STREET AND ENVIRONS

Approximate walking time: 1 hour 30 minutes

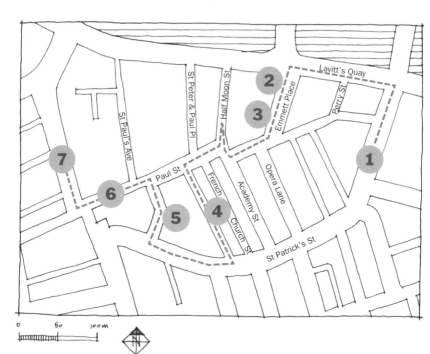

THE WALK: KEY

1 **St Patrick's Street**
2 **Cork Opera House**
3 **Crawford Art Gallery**
4 **Huguenot Cemetery**
5 **Ss Peter and Paul's**
6 **Paul Street**
7 **Cornmarket Street**

THIS PART OF CORK is famous for its shopping but also for its culture. St Patrick's Street is one of Cork's main arteries and is where you will find some of the city's best shops. It is also home to the statue of Fr Mathew, Ireland's great temperance crusader, which overlooks St Patrick's Bridge. This walk also takes in the Cork Opera House and the Crawford Art Gallery, two of Cork's most important cultural venues. Then you will pass the old Huguenot Cemetery and the impressive Gothic church of Ss Peter and Paul, which leads onto Paul Street, crammed with shops, bars and cafés, and finally on to Cornmarket Street, where some of the city's old market buildings can still be found.

1 St Patrick's Street

St Patrick's Street is Cork's most important street, and famous for its shops. It gets its distinctive curve and generous width from the fact that it was originally a waterway. Culverted in the 1780s, when the medieval city began to expand eastwards onto marshland, the street was initially largely residential, but throughout the nineteenth century it gradually took on the more commercial character we see today. Originally lined with waterside warehouses, most of these two-storey buildings have gone. They had outdoor staircases for reaching first-floor offices over the storehouses and you can still see one of them at the corner of Academy Street. The night of 11 December 1920 saw the infamous Burning of Cork. This was when British forces went on a rampage and burned down the City Hall and most of the eastern side of St Patrick's Street. The city worked hard to recover, and some of the finest shopfronts on the street date from the 1920s and 1930s. The street had a further facelift in 2005, with a new look designed by Spanish architect Beth Galli – the distinctive street lighting is supposed to hark back to ships' rigging, a reminder of the street's watery past.

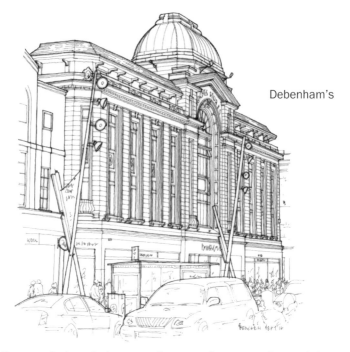

Debenham's

Some of the city's most famous shops are located here. **Debenham's**, which started life as Roches Stores (you can still see the name on the central pediment), is housed in a fine Art Deco building dating from 1927 (one of the many rebuilt after the Burning of Cork). Next door is **Brown Thomas**, a luxury department store that began life as Todd and Company in 1834. Across the street is the iconic Art Deco façade of the old **Savoy Cinema**. Opened in 1932, it not only screened films but was also a venue for live performances and had an excellent restaurant. Sadly, this closed down in 1974 and is now a shop, although the façade still remains to give a flavour of what this atmospheric place used to be like. Three-storey and symmetrical, the façade is covered in a lovely rich golden-coloured faience which contrasts nicely with the blue, although this seems to have faded a little, except where the sign proudly still announces the Savoy to the world.

Presiding at the top of the street is the **statue of Fr Mathew**, the man who founded Ireland's temperance movement in the 1830s. He died in 1856 and this statue, by John Henry Foley, was unveiled in 1864 before a crowd of over 100,000 people. **St Patrick's Bridge** was first built in 1789 as a toll bridge. Traffic crossing over the bridge had to pay; boats sailing under it also had to pay, passing through a portcullis to get into the city. The tolls were scrapped in 1812 and the bridge was destroyed by a flood in 1853 (at least fifteen people died). The current bridge, by John Benson, opened in 1861. The carving at the top of the arches is by a sculptor named Scannell and represents St Patrick, St Bridget, Neptune and three sea goddesses.

DEBENHAM'S
Opening times: Monday to Wednesday and Saturday, 9 a.m. – 6.30 p.m., Thursday, 9 a.m. – 9 p.m., Friday, 9 a.m. – 10 p.m., Sunday, 12 noon – 6.30 p.m.

BROWN THOMAS
Opening times: Monday to Wednesday, 9.30 a.m. – 7 p.m., Thursday and Friday, 9.30 a.m. – 8 p.m., Saturday, 9 a.m. – 7 p.m., Sunday, 11 a.m. – 6 p.m.

FR MATHEW

Fr Theobald Mathew was born at Thomastown Castle, Cashel, County Tipperary in 1790. He was ordained into the priesthood in Dublin in 1813 and moved to Cork the following year where he was chaplain at the County Gaol. He began a school for the poor in 1824 and between 1832 and 1850 built the Holy Trinity Church and Friary (see Holy Trinity Church to St Fin Barre's Cathedral walk). He is best known, however, for founding Ireland's temperance movement in 1838. This was to try and stop alcohol abuse and earned him the nickname the Apostle of Temperance. He died in 1856 and it was decided to build him a memorial. The premature death of sculptor John Hogan in 1858 delayed the project but John Henry Foley took over and the statue on St Patrick's Street was unveiled in 1864 before huge crowds.

2 Cork Opera House

Walk along the river, keeping it to your right, and take the second turn to the left, which will be Emmet Place. You will see the Cork Opera House on your right, along the river. **Emmett Place** was originally a waterway known as King's Dock and in the eighteenth century was where ships from England and Europe would load and unload their cargo, with sailors taking well-earned breaks in the numerous taverns and brothels nearby on Paul Street. By the nineteenth century the city's shipping had moved eastwards and Nelson Place, as it was then called, lay unused. Then, in 1832, the old Custom House was turned into the Royal Cork Institution (now the Crawford Art Gallery). Now called Emmet Place, in honour of the Irish patriot Robert Emmet, it was further improved when the area was pedestrianised, making a spacious civic plaza in front of the gallery and the **Cork Opera House**, which is the largest auditorium in the city, with a capacity of 1,000. It was built in 1955 to replace the old opera house which had been destroyed by fire. Originally part of the **Athenaeum**, which was built in 1853, this was where the first National Exhibition was held at Cork

Cork Opera House

in 1851. The current opera house's entrance façade is glass and faces onto Emmet Place. Inside there are two bars, both of which overlook the river. Despite its name it is mainly used as a theatre, although it regularly hosts live music as well, including performances during the world-renowned annual Choral

Festival and Guinness Jazz Festival. It is also one of the venues for the Cork Film Festival, and hosts the ever popular Christmas pantomimes.

3 Crawford Art Gallery

Next door to the Cork Opera House is the Crawford Art Gallery, Cork's most important art museum and home to a collection of over 2,000 works, including some splendid sculptures. It also hosts a diverse programme of temporary exhibitions and has a fine café and a bookshop. Originally built as the Custom House in 1724, when Emmet Place was a waterway known as King's Dock, it ceased this function when the new Custom House was built downriver in 1815. This charming red-brick and limestone building took on its current shape in the 1880s, when the original Custom House was extended by Arthur Hill for William Horatio Crawford, the wealthy brewer and philanthropist. Initially intended to be a mix of Gothic Revival and Arts and Crafts, the design was toned down to match the existing building so what we see now is a restrained essay in the Queen Anne style (which

Crawford
Art Gallery

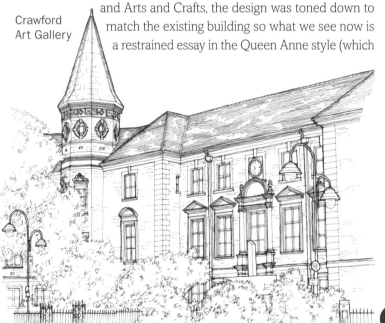

elegantly echoes the lovely red-brick **number 11 Emmet Place** across the road; now a Starbucks, it looks like a doll's house). The gallery was further extended in 2002 by Dutch architect Erick van Egeraat. Behind the gallery, on Half Moon Street, at the back of the Cork Opera House, sits the **Half Moon Theatre**, a small venue popular for live music.

CRAWFORD ART GALLERY
Opening times: Monday – Saturday, 10 a.m. – 5 p.m.
(last entrance 4.45 p.m.), late opening Thursday until 8 p.m.
(last entrance 7.45 p.m.)
Admission: free

4 Huguenot Cemetery

Retrace your steps up Half Moon Street and turn right onto Paul Street, then take the second left onto Carey's Lane and the Huguenot Cemetery will be on your left about halfway down the street. You can see into it through the wrought-iron gateway set into the old stone wall, the last remaining piece of early eighteenth-century masonry in this part of the city. Huguenots were French Protestants forced to flee their homeland because of religious persecution, particularly after the Edict of Nantes, which had protected them, was revoked by Louis XIV in 1685. It is estimated that as many as 200,000 fled. About 5,000 came to Ireland, with 300 or so of them settling in Cork where they quickly became important to the commercial and civic life of the city. They built a

Huguenot Cemetery

church for themselves on French Church Street (originally called Lumley Street, and parallel to Carey's Lane), then in 1733 acquired an almshouse that used to stand where the cemetery now is and turned it into their own burial ground. The French Church (so-called because its services were in French) stopped being a Huguenot place of worship around 1813 when the church was used by Methodists. It was the Methodists who built a large new church here in 1845 before eventually moving out to the Trinity Presbyterian Church on Summerhill North by the end of the century (see the MacCurtain Street to City Hall walk) and their old church was taken over as commercial premises. The last year when anyone was actually buried here was 1901. The cemetery was eventually acquired by Cork City Council in 2007 and turned into a memorial garden. Some of the headstones, both Methodist and Huguenot, can still be seen.

5 Ss Peter and Paul's

Pavilion Cinema

Continue along Carey's Lane and you will come to St Patrick's Street again. Turn right and you will pass the old **Pavilion Cinema**. Like the Savoy, its neighbour up the street, this is now a shop, having closed down in 1989. It also used to contain a restaurant. Opened in 1921, it is not really clear from the façade that this was actually a cinema at all. It is, in fact, rather a fine example of Edwardian-style

Neoclassicism, with Ionic capitals on all columns, pilasters and engaged columns. The clever use of Palladian windows unifies a façade that would otherwise have looked somewhat unbalanced thanks to the right-hand bay being so much lager than the other three – the other three bays are further unified by having the flourish of a shallow circular pediment over the central one. The railings at

FR JOHN MURPHY, NATIVE AMERICAN CHIEF

The building of Ss Peter and Paul's church was largely due to the efforts of one man, the remarkable Fr John Murphy, also known as the Black Eagle of the North. Born in County Cork in 1796, he came from a distinguished Protestant family (his uncle was a bishop, and his nephew went on to found Murphy's Brewery). He was sent to school in England and then joined the East India Company. He later joined the Hudson Bay Company before returning to London to go into business with his brothers. This did not go well so he returned to Canada where he joined a tribe of Native Americans. He lived with them for twelve years, eventually becoming chief and earning himself the name Black Eagle of the North. One day he encountered a French priest in the woods, who asked him for enough flour to make a communion host. Later, when he returned to the same spot, he found a statue of the Virgin Mary (placed there by French Canadian settlers). He saw this as a sign and decided to become a Catholic priest. He sailed to Rome, where he was ordained, and at his ordination he happened to see the old priest who had asked him for flour so many years before in Canada. He moved back to Cork in 1844 and started fundraising for a new parish church. The result was Ss Peter and Paul's, a remarkable building, but not quite so remarkable as the man who built it.

the windows have an almost Art Nouveau sinuosity. It is, in short, a gem of its type, and often missed simply because people so seldom look up when they are shopping. Continue along St Patrick's Street and take the next right onto Ss Peter and Paul's Place and you will see the impressive entrance to **Ss Peter and Paul's** church. This was built as a larger replacement for the nearby Carey's Lane chapel of the 1780s. The competition for its design was won by Edward Welby Pugin (son of the famous A.W.N. Pugin, the architect who led the Gothic Revival movement in England). It opened in 1866 and had twice the capacity of the old church. The entrance is recessed and has some finely carved detailing. The doors' iron hinges are beautifully ornamental, while the great window above is filled with intricate stone tracery. The interior is impressive, giving a feeling of great height, while the side chapels are works of art in themselves. It is a pity that the church's most striking external feature, a belfry intended to soar 70m (230 feet), was never completed.

Ss Peter and Paul's School (former)

6 Paul Street

Continue down Ss Peter and Paul's Place and you will see the former **Ss Peter and Paul's School** towering above you on Paul Street. Designed by Robert Walker, it was built in 1879. The tall façade is asymmetrical and has a hip-roofed tower between the three-storey classroom block and a four-storey residence. The corner is particularly well-handled, with a multi-storey oriel window resting on a single column. For many years this was a neglected part of the city but this old school now looks onto a small new plaza. To the left of the school, further up Paul Street on your right, is the former church of **St Paul's**. Built in 1723, it was deconsecrated in 1950 and used as a warehouse before being turned into a shopping centre in 1997. Set back from the street, a neatly landscaped park nestles behind an impressive set of gates set into weathered stone walls topped by fine railings. The building itself is a simple Neoclassical style, with five arched windows over smaller square windows and doors. A glass extension links it to the rest of the shopping centre. **Paul Street** used to be home to craftsmen like plumbers, tinsmiths and shoemakers; it also had a number of taverns and brothels catering to the sailors who used to come to King's Dock (as Emmet Place was known in the eighteenth century). The nineteenth century saw many of these houses turn into tenements. These were cleared in the 1930s and the street is now known for its shops and restaurants, including **Waterstones** bookshop, the front of which opens onto St Patrick's Street, and **The Woodford**, originally a wine and spirit merchants founded in 1750, this delightful five-storey warehouse is now home to an atmospheric restaurant and bar.

••

DID YOU KNOW?

Punishment stocks used to be located outside the former St Paul's church. These were where criminals had their hands or feet locked in a board for a certain period of time and passers-by would sometimes throw rotten vegetables at them. These were still here (although not in use) as late as the 1930s.

7 Cornmarket Street

Continue along Paul Street and you will come out onto Cornmarket Street. Across the road sits a rather ramshackle-looking Neoclassical building. This was the city's **Corn Market** and thought to be designed by Italian architect Alessandro Galilei in 1740 (also responsible for Castletown House in County Kildare). It is a large, single-storey symmetrical building in a light grey limestone. Consisting of three pedimented ranges, the central one is the tallest, with three arches flanked by Tuscan engaged columns topped by a clock. It is now home to a number of bars and restaurants, whose tables are laid out on the pavement overlooking the street. If you want a more traditional type of pub, then leave the old Corn Market by turning left and cross the street, then, just where it begins to curve to the right, you will see **Dennehy's**, a pleasant old-world place with lots of charm, and the perfect place to take a break. Finally, slightly further up Cornmarket Street on your right, at numbers 44 to 45, you will see the old **St Peter's Market**, now home to a restaurant and wine bar. This part of the street was originally part of Coal Quay which, like so many other streets in this part of town, was originally a waterway. St Peter's Market was more commonly known as the Irish Market (to distinguish it from the English Market on Grand Parade), and this is where people from the surrounding countryside would come to sell their wares, giving it the nickname Paddy's Market.

Link to the Grand Parade walk:
Leave St Peter's Market by retracing your steps down Cornmarket Street and continue until you come to the corner of Castle Street. Take a left and an immediate right and you will be on Grand Parade.

GRAND PARADE

Approximate walking time: 30 minutes

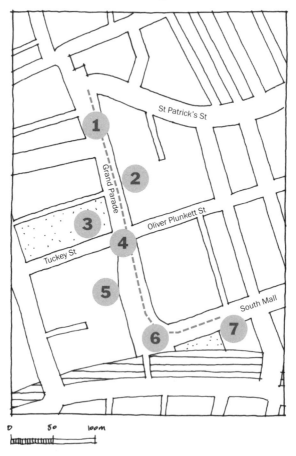

THE WALK: KEY

1 **Grand Parade**

2 **English Market**

3 **Bishop Lucey Park**

4 **Berwick Fountain**

5 **City Library**

6 **National Monument**

7 **The Electric**

G RAND PARADE is by far the shortest walk in the book, but, as its name suggests, one of the most important streets in the city. Home to some of Cork's most important tourist attractions, including the impressive National Monument and the charming Berwick Fountain, it is also where you will find the popular Bishop Lucey Park, which has the remains of some of Cork's medieval city walls. Next to the park sits the City Library, an unashamedly Modernist construction. The walk ends at The Electric, a seafood restaurant and bar housed in a delightful Art Deco building overlooking the southern and fast-moving channel of the River Lee, and an excellent place for a break. The walk starts, however, with a stroll through Cork's world-famous English Market, one of the best places in the whole country for fresh produce (and home to the lovely Farmgate Café, On the Pig's Back charcuterie and many more).

1 Grand Parade

Grand Parade is one of the most important shopping streets in the city, and has been since the Victorian era when it was home to some of Cork's finest and most fashionable shops. It was particularly well known for its food and drink. This is where the old medieval city began to expand eastwards from the middle of the eighteenth century. By 1800 Grand Parade had assumed the shape you see today and, like St Patrick's Street, owes its generous width (particularly its southern end) to the fact that it was once a waterway. The northern end is narrower but still manages to feel almost like a plaza. To your left is a fine, four-storey Neoclassical building which curves confidently around the corner onto St Patrick's Street. Designed by W.H. Hill around 1890, it is now home to a McDonald's but if you look upwards you can still see the sign for **Woodford Bourne and Company**, a famous Victorian emporium founded in Falconer's Lane in 1750. (It had a number of different names before ending up as Woodford Bourne and Company in the nineteenth century.) Facing this across the plaza is **Queen's Old Castle**. It may be hard to believe when looking at this building now, but this used to be one of Cork's best-known department stores. It is a rather oddly proportioned Neoclassical building but the two-storey fluted Doric entrance is rather fine. This sits under a pediment featuring a clock. The arched upper-storey windows are large and bright and make the whole thing seem an odd mix of Victorian and Neoclassical styles. The shop signs, unfortunately, obscure the column capitals on the ground floor. The building's name is also rather odd but that is because it is very ancient. Cork's coat of arms portrays a ship sailing between two towers – the medieval city's water gate. Queen's Old Castle is located where the northern tower of this gate sat. Known as Queen's Castle (the southern one was King's Castle) it does not seem to have left any trace, apart from the name. Further down Grand Parade, on your right, is Washington Street, the corners of which have long had specific names. **Finn's Corner** is named after a company established here in 1858, while **Singer's Corner** (you can still see the name of the famous sewing-machine manufacturer based here since 1875 on the façade) has three energetically decorated upper floors.

••

DID YOU KNOW?

Woodford Bourne and Company imported so much wine into Ireland in the nineteenth century that it had to keep its own customs officer working full-time.

2 English Market

Continue down Grand Parade and you will see **the Capitol** on your left, an elegant, large-scale shopping complex that stretches back

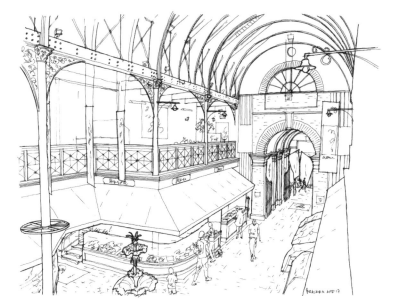

English Market

from Grand Parade and opens out onto neighbouring St Patrick's Street. It takes its name from the old Capitol cinema, which opened here in 1947, when it replaced Grant's furniture and clothes shop, which had been destroyed by fire in 1942. Despite being converted into a multiplex in 1989, the Capitol closed down in 2005.

Next door to the Capitol is **the English Market**. This attractively symmetrical façade, with arched entrances on either side, was designed by John Benson and is a jaunty Victorian take on the Neoclassical style. Its most recent restoration saw it painted a bright and pleasing range of greens (appropriate for a market specialising in vegetables, among other things). A covered market was established here in 1788 and takes its name from the fact that it had a largely Protestant (or 'English') clientele. Catholics were not banned, but as they tended to be poorer they went to the cheaper Irish (or St Peter's) Market on nearby Coal Quay (now Cornmarket Street – see the St Patrick's Street and Environs walk). The English Market's present structure (which stretches all the way back to Prince's Street) dates from 1840 but was only completed in 1862, when the Prince's Street extension was added to cover an open-air market. This extension has a delightful two-storey top-lit atrium ringed with galleries overlooking a decorative cast-iron fountain. This is linked to Prince's Street via a passageway that leads under a double-height archway at the centre of a particularly fine symmetrical Byzantine façade which features a pedimented Diocletian window. The rest of the market is single storey and the whole complex is, in short, a gem: attractive, well-designed and pleasant to be in. Cork is justifiably renowned for its food: both the city and county have world-class reputations when it comes to produce and the restaurants in which to eat it. The English Market is an absolute haven for food lovers, with a huge variety of stalls crammed with fantastic fresh produce from a wide variety of local producers, everything from artisan butchers and bakers to cheese- and fishmongers. Brands to look out for are Tom Durcan's spiced beef, Frank Hederman's smoked fish, O'Flynn's gourmet sausages, Declan Ryan's Arbutus Bread and Toonsbridge Dairy buffalo mozzarella. You could lose yourself for hours just browsing and sampling their wares, but whatever you do, make sure you take time to venture upstairs and try some of the delicious food in the excellent **Farmgate Café**.

ENGLISH MARKET

Opening times: Monday – Saturday, 8 a.m. – 6 p.m
(closed bank holidays)
Admission: free

FARMGATE CAFÉ

Opening times: Monday – Saturday, 8.30 a.m. – 5 p.m.
(closed bank holidays)
Admission: free

DID YOU KNOW?
Queen Elizabeth II visited the English Market during her historic visit to Ireland in 2011.

3 Bishop Lucey Park

Almost opposite the English Market is Bishop Lucey Park. Opened in 1985, during the 800th anniversary of Cork's city status, it is named after a popular Catholic Bishop, Cornelius Lucey, who served the city for more than 30 years. One of the few green spaces in the city centre, it is popular with office workers who, if the weather is fine, have lunch here (many of them buy their food at the English Market across the street). In the run-up to Christmas the park is transformed into a Winter Wonderland, delightful for small children (and their parents); a **Christmas Market** is also held outside the main entrance, adding to the festive atmosphere. The park's unusual double gate was originally the entrance to a corn market on Anglesea Street, salvaged when it was demolished and re-erected here. It is rather fine, in a heavy Romanesque style, with light-coloured limestone arches springing from a central thick engaged column. A small portion of red limestone wall can be seen under a heave entablature, with massive dentils. Inside, the park is pleasantly and simply landscaped and you can see a portion of the old **medieval city wall** which was uncovered in 1984 when the park was being laid out. Parts of this wall date back to the thirteenth century and you can also see signs of where it was repaired in the seventeenth.

Gateway, Bishop
Lucey Park

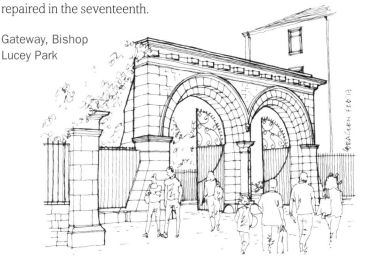

Thought to have stood around 6m (20 feet) tall, once the city began to expand eastwards the wall was no longer useful and its stones were carried off by people who found them useful for building material. The park is also home to two notable sculptures: **The Onion Seller**, by Seamus Murphy, a tribute to street traders from nearby Cornmarket Street; and a **bronze fountain** featuring eight swans by John Behan, the swans symbolising the number of centuries since Cork's establishment as a city.

4 Berwick Fountain

Wander Bishop Lucey Park at will and go back out onto Grand Parade and turn right. Sitting at the crossroads of Tuckey Street is the Berwick Fountain, one of the few public fountains in the city. Designed by John Benson in 1860, it is named after Walter Berwick, a popular judge who presented it to the city because he was delighted to receive so many congratulations on his appointment to the judgeship in 1859. Located near the site of Tuckey's Bridge (built when Grand Parade was a waterway), the fountain's moulded limestone base is basically a square with four circular projections. The central three-tier portion sports dolphins with tails intertwined. When the street was refurbished in 2006 the fountain was temporarily disassembled for safekeeping and reassembled the following year on a spot close to its original location.

5 City Library

Just beyond the Berwick Fountain Grand Parade begins to widen, indicating that it was originally an important waterway before being culverted. The large block of the City Library, on your right, is in an unashamedly Modernist style and perhaps not to everyone's taste. It is, however, due to receive a facelift, which should make it seem

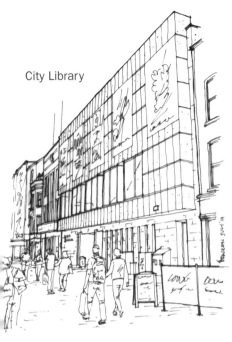
City Library

lighter as there will be more glass on the façade (something that will enliven the heavy façade, which has so few windows – a pity for a building facing onto one of Cork's liveliest streets). The redesign will still incorporate the Celtic-style Art Deco building next door. The City Library is home to Cork's largest collection of books and periodicals, and also hosts numerous exhibitions, talks and performances in the Thomas Davis Room. In 2004 the Music Room was renamed in honour of one of Ireland's best-known musicians, Rory Gallagher, a singer-songwriter born in County Donegal but brought up in Cork, who was a gifted rock guitarist and famous for his charismatic performances (he died in 1995 aged 47). The Rory Gallagher Music Room houses an extensive collection of music books, CDs, DVDs, and musical scores in a variety of genres, including classical, jazz, world, rock, pop, traditional and contemporary. In 2015 a collection of previously unseen photographs of Rory on tour with his band Taste went on permanent display after being kindly donated by photographer Stephen Smith.

• •

DID YOU KNOW?

It is appropriate that Rory Gallagher is commemorated in a library as he was a voracious reader, with a particular fondness for crime novels, which he brought on tour with him. They even used to inspire his songwriting.

6 National Monument

Towards the end of Grand Parade stands Dominic Coakley's magnificent National Monument, an imposing Gothic shrine to those who died fighting for Irish freedom in the rebellions of 1798, 1803, 1848 and 1867. Funds raised by the Cork Young Ireland Society helped pay for it and it replaces an equestrian statue of George II (which mysteriously ended up in the river in 1862). The monument features figures of Theobald Wolfe Tone, Thomas Davis, Peter O'Neill Crowley and Michael Dwyer, as well as the Mother Erin, for whom they were all fighting. These were sculpted by John Francis Davis. The monument was unveiled on St Patrick's Day 1906, with (appropriately enough) a grand parade up the street. Thousands lined the route and after the unveiling there were speeches by, among others, Jeremiah O'Donovan Rossa and Charles Guilfoyle Doran. Facing the monument on the right-hand (western) side of the street are a number of **bow-fronted Georgian houses** with slate-clad façades. These were built using brick that came to Cork as ballast in merchant ships. Slate is more usually used on roofs but can be seen on walls in a number of Ireland's coastal towns as it is an excellent waterproof material.

National Monument

DID YOU KNOW?

Grand Parade was originally known in Irish as *Sráid an Chapaill Bhuí* (Street of the Yellow Horse). This was because of the imposing equestrian statue of George II located where the National Monument now stands. It ended up in the river in 1862, and even though it was fished out, it never regained its position.

7 The Electric

To the left of the National Monument is a small triangular park overlooking the River Lee, at the centre of which stands another memorial, a simple and somewhat forlorn-looking **War Memorial**, dedicated to those from Cork who died fighting in both world wars. It consists of an obelisk featuring a bas-relief of a soldier in First World War uniform.

The Electric

His rifle is pointed downwards and he stands in a sombre posture under a wreath. The plaque on the plinth underneath notes that the monument was paid for by public subscription in memory of comrades of the Ex-Servicemen's Club who died in the two world wars. Facing onto this small space is **The Electric**, a popular bar and restaurant specialising in seafood. Housed in an imaginatively renovated Art Deco building, its three façades face onto three very different views: South Mall; the small park, with its war memorial; and the River Lee. The building has been painted beige with brown trim around jazzy turquoise panels between the windows. It is also a popular place to hang out for a drink. The riverside bar on the first floor has panoramic views of Holy Trinity Church and St Fin Barre's Cathedral, as well as of the river, which cascades over a weir here. It is a wonderful place to stop and take a well-deserved rest, or maybe even some refreshments.

Link to the Holy Trinity Church to St Fin Barre's Cathedral walk:
Leave The Electric by turning right onto South Mall. Then take the next right onto Parliament Street, then left onto Fr Mathew Quay and you will see Holy Trinity Church ahead of you overlooking the river.

HOLY TRINITY CHURCH TO ST FIN BARRE'S CATHEDRAL

Approximate walking time: 2 hours

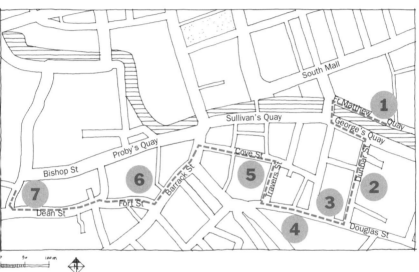

THE WALK: KEY

1 **Holy Trinity Church**
2 **St Finbarr's South**
3 **Red Abbey**
4 **Nano Nagle Place**
5 **St Nicholas (former)**
6 **Elizabeth Fort**
7 **St Fin Barre's Cathedral**

T HIS WALK TAKES YOU through the south of the city, an area that contains some of Cork's most magnificent churches, beginning with the Holy Trinity Church. You will visit St Finbarr's South, the former church of St Nicholas, and Cork's most iconic religious building, St Fin Barre's Cathedral. A hilly part of the city, there are a number of stepped streets, as well as old buildings that took advantage of the extra height the hills afforded, such as the Red Abbey (now a ruin) and the Elizabeth Fort, which guarded the old medieval city. There is also a fascinating new heritage centre dedicated to Nano Nagle housed in the buildings of the school she founded.

1 Holy Trinity Church

This impressive church and friary was founded by Fr Mathew, Apostle of Temperance, in the 1820s and is the work of several different architects. George Pain was responsible for the original design in 1825 but building proved slow, particularly because of the difficulty of the riverside site, which needed extra foundations. Construction was further delayed by the Great Famine in the 1840s but began once again under architect William Atkins in the 1850s. The church's signature Gothic portico and spire were not built until 1889–1891 and were, in fact, designed by yet another architect, Dominic Coakely, who won the competition (he also designed the nearby National Monument – see the Grand Parade walk). Coakely reduced the height of Pain's original design (to save costs) but stayed true to his vision by creating this remarkably airy structure that seems to float above the quayside. Consisting of three very lofty arches resting on octagonal piers, between these sit the rather unusual feature of a stone screen forming a sort of porch for the central doorway. The tower is two-storey and has an open parapet of tracery with a spire above. The tower's upper storey and the lower portion of the spire are open, and it is this that gives them

Holy Trinity Church

the startling combination of towering strength and soaring lightness. A new sanctuary was built here in 1906, adding to the length of the church. Its interior was also altered by George Ashlin around 1908, obliterating most of Atkins' earlier work. Adjoining the church is a **monastery** of limestone and red brick. This was built by Robert Walker in 1888. On the other side of the church you will find **Friary Lane**, named after the Capuchins' original chapel. It was in this chapel that Fr Mathew began his Temperance Movement in 1838.

2 St Finbarr's South

Leave Holy Trinity Church and go back up Fr Mathew Quay. Turn left over **Parliament Bridge**, a sturdily elegant structure built in 1806 to replace an earlier bridge that had been destroyed by a flood. Its gracious limestone arch is topped by a colonnaded balustrade. Turn left onto George's Quay, and then right onto Dunbar Street and you will come to St Finbarr's South on your left. This large plain church was the first Catholic place of worship built in the city after the Reformation. Also known as the South Chapel, it was built in

JOHN HOGAN

One of Ireland's most talented and best-known sculptors was born in Tallow, County Waterford in 1800. His family moved to Cork when he was ten and lived not far from St Finbarr's South, on Cove Street. His first job, as a young teenager, was clerk to a solicitor, which he disliked. Then he began an apprenticeship to architect Thomas Deane (Hogan's father worked as a foreman for the Deanes). His talent for drawing and carving soon got him spotted (it was Deane who gave the young Hogan his first set of chisels). Funds were raised and he was sent to Rome to train as a sculptor in 1823. He stayed in Italy until 1848 when he returned to Ireland with his Italian wife but his health soon began to decline and he died in 1858. He is buried in Glasnevin Cemetery, Dublin and his grave is marked by a simple slab of stone marked HOGAN. His best-known works include *The Sleeping Shepherd*, *The Drunken Faun*, and *The Dead Christ*, all of which feature slender yet athletic-looking young men (or mythical creatures) lying (or sprawled) in sleep, stupor or death. *The Dead Christ* in St Finbarr's South is carved from Carrara marble and dates from 1833. It is the second version of the statue (the first, dating from 1829, is in St Theresa's, Dublin, while the third (from 1854) is in the Basilica of St John the Baptist, Newfoundland).

1766 and extended twice in the nineteenth century, once in 1809, when its L-shaped plan was extended into the more usual cross shape, and again in 1866, when this plan was further extended. A new altar was installed in 1873 and incorporates John Hogan's beautiful sculpture **The Dead Christ**, a serene life-size statue in white Carrara marble (the model for which was the playboy son of a wealthy Cork merchant named Duncan, who repented of his ways and allowed his hair to grow for months so that he could look sufficiently Christ-like). Daniel O'Connell attended Mass here a number of times in the late 1820s and the chapel yard contains fragments of old tombstones originally belonging to the nearby ruined Red Abbey.

The Dead Christ

3 Red Abbey

Continue up Dunbar Street and turn right onto Douglas Street and you will see the ruined bell tower of the old Red Abbey on your right. This 20m (65-foot) tower is a national monument and all that remains of an Augustinian Abbey founded here around 1280. The tower was completed sometime around 1450 and is one of the last remaining medieval structures still standing in Cork. Located outside the eastern walls of the medieval city, the abbey was wealthy, owning two watermills and a salmon fishery near Southgate Bridge. Henry VIII suppressed the monasteries in the 1540s, and a survey carried out at that time lists it as having a dormitory, hall, buttery, kitchen, cloister, six rooms and six cellars, as well as a small orchard and three small gardens, one of which included a cemetery. Despite the suppression, the Augustinians managed to remain here until 1641 (the Chinese saying 'the mountains are high and the king is far away' might be appropriate here). English monasteries were not treated so leniently, and many of them subsequently got turned into stately homes like Woburn Abbey in Bedfordshire (probably the inspiration for TV's *Downton Abbey*). Cromwell was more thorough than Henry, however, and got rid of the monasteries. The abbey was sold off to local merchants in the second half of the seventeenth century. The tower was then used as a place from which to bombard the city below during the Siege of Cork in 1690. The buildings were then used as a sugar refinery from the middle of the eighteenth century, but these burned down in 1799 and the shell was demolished, all except for the tower, which has been looked after by Cork City Council since 1951.

The Augustinians were not to be beaten, however. They returned to Cork in the 1740s, establishing themselves just off Liberty Street and built a new friary on what is now Washington Street in 1788 (see the Medieval City chapter). This is now the site of St Augustine's, the church they built in the 1940s.

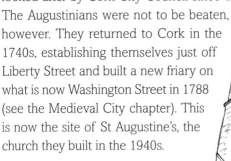

. . . .

DID YOU KNOW?
Red Abbey got its name from the red sandstone used in its construction.

Red Abbey
tower

4 Nano Nagle Place

Continue along Douglas Street, which turns into Abbey Street, and you will come to Nano Nagle Place on your left. Formerly the South Presentation Convent, this labyrinth of Victorian institutional buildings is built in Cork's trademark red brick and limestone and once housed a school and chapel. It was founded by Nano Nagle, a wealthy eighteenth-century Catholic woman who became an educational pioneer by teaching the poor of the city in a mud cabin. She went on to found a religious order, the Presentation Sisters, which now has schools all over the world. These beautifully restored buildings are now home to a heritage centre that tells the story of Nano Nagle's life, and the work of the order she founded. You can also learn the fascinating history of eighteenth-century Cork. The complex also includes exhibition space, a design store and a garden café tucked away in its secret little Italianate garden, which is where you can also find the tomb of the woman who started it all.

NANO NAGLE PLACE
Opening times: Daily 10 a.m. – 5 p.m.
Admission: free

DID YOU KNOW?
The great Irish short-story writer Frank O'Connor was born on Douglas Street in 1903.

5 St Nicholas (former)

Continue up Abbey Street and take a right down Travers Street. Turn left onto Cove Street and the former church of St Nicholas will be on your left, through a gate and up a winding driveway. This is one of the finest Gothic churches in the city. Standing near the

Nicholas Church Lane

site of the ancient Church of St Bridget, there has been a church here since medieval times. Damaged during the Siege of Cork in 1690, a Neoclassical structure was built in 1720 but this was struck by lightning six years later. Rebuilt in 1836 in the Gothic style by Joseph Welland, it was not consecrated until 1850, which is when William Atkins added the handsome tower and steeple. (Atkins had just lost out on winning the competition for nearby St Fin Barre's Cathedral and clearly decided to have a little fun here.) The massing of the church and spire is handled with masterly assurance and particularly effective when seen from the approaching driveway that winds its way up the hill. Deconsecrated in the 1990s, it is now home to the probation service.

St Nicholas
(former)

6 Elizabeth Fort

Continue along Cove Street and turn left onto **Barrack Street**. This area is one of the oldest of the city and was always a popular place to go out, especially with barracks located nearby. It is home to two pleasant pubs: **Tom Barry's** is cosy in winter with its fireplace and has a beer garden for the all-too-brief Irish summers (it also hosts live music every Thursday), while **The Gateway** is reputed to be the oldest pub in the city and is popular with students. Continue up Barrack Street and turn right onto Fort Street and you will be at the **Elizabeth Fort**. This star-shaped fort, named after Queen Elizabeth I, was built in 1601 to keep an eye on Cork after a siege of the city earlier that year. Initially constructed of timber and earth, it was dismantled by locals when James I came to the throne two years later. The locals came to regret this action, however, as the massive replacement, built of stone in 1626, had to be paid for by the citizens of Cork. It was used as a fortress and barracks. A second barracks was built across the street in 1698. Both of these closed down when a new barracks was built on the north side of the city in 1806. The fort then underwent a variety of uses, including a women's prison, a fever hospital and, eventually, a police barracks for the Royal Irish Constabulary (RIC). It was used as a base for the notorious Black and Tans during Ireland's War of Independence and all the buildings inside were burned down during the Civil War that followed. It then saw new use by the Garda Síochána (Irish police force), who built the quaint little houses, striking an unexpectedly suburban note in this otherwise sombre old building. No longer used by the police, it is now a fascinating museum and has ramparts that command stunning views of the city.

ELIZABETH FORT
Opening times: Tuesday – Saturday, 10 a.m. – 5 p.m., Sunday, 12 noon – 5 p.m. (guided tours 1 p.m.)
Admission charges

THE SIEGE OF CORK, 1690

When James II came to the throne of England in 1685 he upset Protestant sensibilities by advocating religious tolerance for Catholics (he was himself a Catholic). No one minded too much because his daughter Mary, a Protestant, was heir to the throne. All that changed, however, when James had a son, Charles, in 1688 and it looked like England would once again be ruled by a Catholic dynasty. A group of nobles clubbed together and invited Prince William of Orange to come to England. Prince William was Stadhouder (military leader) of the United Provinces (the Netherlands) and feared an Anglo-French alliance that might threaten his own country's security. He landed in England in 1688 and quickly routed James II's forces. However, Ireland (staunchly Catholic) supported the king and the theatre of war moved here. Meanwhile, William and his wife Mary (James's daughter) were declared King William III and Queen Mary II in 1689. This was known as the Glorious Revolution because it was bloodless – at least in England; what happened in Ireland was another story. Fighting continued, with sieges of Derry and Cork in 1690 and the Battle of the Boyne that same year, after which James finally admitted defeat and hostilities ended with the Treaty of Limerick in 1691. The Glorious Revolution ended any chance of a Catholic ever becoming king of England (there are still laws today to prevent this). It also ushered in an era of persecution for Catholics (thanks to what were known as the Penal Laws) that lasted well over a century until Catholic Liberation was ushered in by Daniel O'Connell in 1829.

Leave the Elizabeth Fort by turning right onto Fort Street and follow it as it turns into Dean Street, then take a right onto Bishop Street and you will see St Fin Barre's Cathedral on your right. This magnificent cathedral dominates the skyline of Cork with its three spires – the massing of these is particularly well handled and clearly designed to be seen from a distance. Sited above the River Lee on what are believed to be the foundations of St Fin Barre's monastery,

St Fin Barre's
Cathedral

BRACKEN APR '17

this Protestant place of worship is in a French Gothic style, although some of its decorative elements hark back to Ireland's medieval past. Designed by William Burgess, who won the competition to replace an older and rather run-down church, the foundation was laid in 1865 and the church consecrated five years later, with the towers and spires being completed by 1876. It is a masterpiece, with echoes of medieval French cathedrals such as Chartres, Noyon and Laon, yet it has a gingerbread charm all its own. It is cruciform in shape, with a lofty nave, aisled at either side and widening into twin transepts that terminate in a magnificent semicircular apse. One of the most impressive features of the building is its West Entrance, which consists of three deep-set doorways featuring elaborate carving. This is clearly influenced by medieval French cathedrals, with the various statues narrating the stories of the Bible from the Creation to Judgement Day (you can see the Four Evangelists around the central rose window, and Christ seated in judgement in the pediment above). The cathedral's bells were retained from the earlier church, and the chancel roof features a life-size gilded archangel blowing a trumpet, a gift from Burgess in 1870 to commemorate the death of his daughter. The **Cork Arts Collective**, set up in 1985, is based in the cathedral's grounds and organises forums and exhibitions to promote the work of local artists. The **Bishop's Palace** across the road from the cathedral is a rather fine Georgian mansion designed by Thomas Ivory in the eighteenth century.

··

DID YOU KNOW?

The organ of St Fin Barre's Cathedral was originally located over the central entrance but is now under the chancel floor, making it the only underground church organ in the world.

ST FINBARR

St Finbarr is Cork's patron saint and founded a
monastery and school here in the early seventh century.
Thought to have been born near Innishannon in County
Cork sometime in the sixth century, he was the son of a
metalworker called Amairgen who had come from the
west of Ireland to work at the court of one of the kings
in the Munster area. Unwittingly, he had an illicit
relationship with one of the king's handmaidens and
when it was discovered she was pregnant they were
both condemned to death. Before they could be cast
into the fire, the child in her womb pleaded for mercy,
which was granted; then again, immediately after being
born, the child spoke to ask for his parents' freedom,
which the king gladly granted. The family moved to
near Macroom and called their child Loan of the Fair
Hair. When he was seven he was spotted by three holy
men from Leinster – Brendan, Lochan and Fidach –
who recognised his special powers. He studied under
them, and others, before returning to Cork around 600,
now named Finbarr, to found a place of worship and
education. The precise location of his monastery has
never been ascertained, although it is thought to be at
Gill Abbey, somewhere between St Fin Barre's
Cathedral and University College Cork, two institutions
that claim descent from this medieval miracle worker.
(He also founded another monastery at Gougane Barra,
near Macroom in West Cork.) St Finbarr died around
630, but his monastery continued to grow in strength
and importance, even during the Viking invasions in the
ninth century, but it was destroyed in the burning of
Cork in 1081.

ST FIN BARRE'S CATHEDRAL

Opening times: Monday – Saturday, 9.30 a.m. – 5.30 p.m., Sunday, 12.45 – 2.30 p.m. and 4.30 – 5.30 p.m. (April to October); Monday – Saturday, 9.30 a.m. – 5.30 p.m. (November to March)

Admission charges

. . . .

DID YOU KNOW?

The committee in charge of overseeing the rebuilding of St Fin Barre's Cathedral objected to the idea of some of the statues being naked (the risen dead) so they were carved with their clothes on instead.

Legend has it that the people of Cork will be the first to get into heaven because the gilded archangel on top of St Fin Barre's Cathedral will blow his trumpet to give advance warning on Judgement Day.

Link to the Medieval City walk:
Leave St Fin Barre's Cathedral by turning right onto Bishop Street, then continue as this turns into Sharman Crawford Street and the CIT Crawford College of Art and Design will be on your left.

MEDIEVAL CITY

Approximate walking time: 2 hours

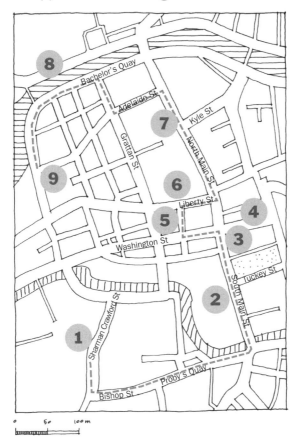

THE WALK: KEY

1 **CIT Crawford College of Art and Design**

2 **Beamish and Crawford (former)**

3 **Triskel Christchurch**

4 **St Augustine's**

5 **Courthouse**

6 **St Francis's**

7 **St Peter's (former)**

8 **North Mall**

9 **Mercy Hospital**

T HIS IS THE MEDIEVAL HEART of Cork, the walled city that dates from the thirteenth century. The walls have long gone but the dense street pattern remains, even though there is not much evidence of medieval architecture on it. There are a number of fine churches, however, including St Augustine's and St Francis's; as well as two others, St Peter's and Triskel Christchurch, which have been converted into cultural centres. Administratively important, this part of town is where you will find the imposing Courthouse and the former Mayor's House (now the Mercy Hospital). North Mall, just across the northern channel of the River Lee, was one of the city's most fashionable addresses, and there also used to be a number of breweries here. The huge complex of Beamish and Crawford's former brewery has some lovely Victorian Tudor architecture, whereas the CIT Crawford College of Art and Design, which is where this walk begins, is a lovely Edwardian building which takes its name from one of these famous brewers.

1 CIT Crawford College of Art and Design

The CIT Crawford College of Art and Design on Sharman Crawford Street is a lovely Edwardian building built as the Crawford Municipal Technical Institute by Cork architect Samuel Hill in 1912. It replaced the old Arnott's Brewery, which was purchased by Murphy's Brewery in 1901. This area used to be quite industrial, with not just brewing, but distilling, milling and sugar refining all taking place here from the eighteenth century onwards. The area was one of the many islands that formed part of what was the Great Marsh of Munster. Known as Holy Island, it was home to a Dominican abbey called St Mary's of the Isle. James II was a guest here in 1689. Then, when the religious order of the Mercy Sisters moved here in 1852, they called their new Convent **St Marie's of the Isle**. They built a new and beautiful Gothic complex, complete with spire, which was located further down the street on the right-hand side. Designed by William Atkins, the chapel was finally completed in 1869. Retrace your steps down Sharman Crawford Street and turn left onto Bishop Street and you will pass the old **stable block** of the Beamish and Crawford brewery, one of the most accomplished industrial buildings in the city (see the Architectural Styles chapter for an illustration). Built in 1902 by Houston and Houston of London, this is a playful little building in the Arts and Crafts style. A row of windows sits in a red-brick wall over beautifully detailed limestone. The mansard roof is pierced by large ventilation stacks topped by concave cowls. The central portion, over the front door, is raised and features timber and plaster detailing, as does the pretty little gate lodge, which has an overhanging upper floor and diagonally positioned chimneys.

2 Beamish and Crawford (former)

Continue along Bishop Street, which turns into Proby's Quay, then take a left onto **Southgate Bridge**. Constructed in 1713, this is Cork's oldest bridge and led to the medieval city's South Gate. Cork County Gaol used to be located here. Built in 1730, it was where the heads of criminals were displayed on spikes. Over the bridge and you are on South Main Street, the main thoroughfare through the medieval city. To your left is the vast complex of the former brewery **Beamish and Crawford**, once the largest industrial concern in the city centre. It closed down in 2009 but there are plans to develop the site, which covers nearly 2.5 hectares (5 acres). A brewery was begun here in 1782 and was purchased by William Beamish and William Crawford soon after (in 1791). Porter began to be produced the following year and it was for many years Ireland's largest brewery (until 1833, when Dublin's Guinness took over). Beamish and Crawford kept on growing here, however, and had reached its greatest extent by the 1880s. Most of the buildings

Beamish and Crawford (former)

on the western side of this site are eighteenth century, but the magnificent Victorian Tudor block you can see overlooking the yard is from the nineteenth. Continue up South Main Street and you will pass the small (and optimistically named) **Sober Lane** on your right. Keep going and at the corner of Tuckey Street you will see **The Oval**, an atmospheric pub housed in a lovely three-storey Arts and Crafts corner building that seems not to have been touched since before the First World War. At numbers 25–27 Tuckey Street you will find the **Masonic Hall**, home to the Provincial Grand Lodge of Munster, which was established in Cork in 1723, making it the oldest lodge in the country (they used to meet at a tavern at Southgate Bridge). The building fortunately survived a fire in 1971 so still has most of its historical regalia, as well as some of the stalls from the old St Fin Barre's Cathedral.

••

DID YOU KNOW?

Eighteenth-century residents of South Main Street used to complain about the heads displayed on spikes in front of Southgate Gaol, particularly when, on a windy day, they would be blown up the street.

Cork Strolls

90

3 Triskel Christchurch

Continue up South Main Street and you will pass the rear entrance to Bishop Lucey Park on your right and Triskel Christchurch will be just beside the park. There has been a church on this site for a thousand years. The first Christ Church was built by the Danes, the second by the Anglo-Normans. All but destroyed in the Siege of Cork in 1690, a third, in a stripped-down

Triskel Christchurch

Neoclassical style, was built in 1726. It used to have a 40m (136-foot) tower but this had to be taken down in 1810 when it began to lean to one side. The fine Ionic portico was added by the Pain brothers in 1828, when they also remodelled the interior, introducing scagliola (a substitute for marble) to Ireland for the first time. Deconsecrated in 1978, it is now an arts centre housing a 100-seater theatre, a gallery space, a workshop and a bar and restaurant. Look out for the tomb of the so-called 'modest man', a former Mayor of Cork. There is also a poignant stained-glass window commemorating the 4,000 men from Cork who died fighting in the First World War; it features David confronting Goliath.

TRISKEL CHRISTCHURCH

Opening times: Tuesday – Saturday, 10 a.m. – 4 p.m. (cultural events take place on Sundays and weekday evenings)

Admission: free (some events have charges)

Medieval City

DID YOU KNOW?

Triskel Christchurch's organ was a gift to the church from Sir Francis Drake. He found it among the treasure seized from a Spanish galleon. Intended as a gift from the King of Spain to the people of Mexico, it was made in Leipzig, Germany.

4 St Augustine's

Continue up South Main Street and you will pass Hanover Street on your left. Most people think of the name Waterford when they think of Irish crystal, but there used to be a number of excellent glassmakers located in Cork. In fact, there were as many as eleven **glass factories** located around Hanover Street and nearby Wandesford Quay in 1825. The Cork Glass Company, The Waterloo Glass Company and The Terrace Glass Company were the best known; sadly, a combination of punitive English tariffs and self-destructive industrial action on the part of the glass-workers themselves spelled the end of the industry by the middle of the nineteenth century. Hanover Street was also where there used to be a **Public Dispensary**. Established in 1787, it was to provide healthcare for the poor. Continue up South Main Street and take a right onto Washington Street and you will see **St Augustine's** on your left. This remarkable-looking building, with its tall thin arched windows, began life as a modest chapel on nearby Brunswick Street (the Augustinians had previously owned the Red Abbey but were forced to sell when the Penal Laws began to bite in the seventeenth century – see the Holy Trinity Church to St Fin Barre's Cathedral walk). They built themselves a priory in 1872 and began to make plans for a larger church, deciding to build a new one rather than simply enlarge the existing. Plans did not get under way until 1937, and were then delayed due to the Second World War because of the difficulty in getting building materials. Much of the stonework actually came from the defunct ten-arch Mallow Viaduct, and it is one of the building's defining features (it being such an otherwise plain façade). The Washington Street entrance is in the Italian Renaissance style and well carved, but there was also supposed to be a 60m (200-foot) bell tower along with a more elaborate entrance on Grand Parade, but, due to lack of funds, these were never built.

5 Courthouse

Retrace your steps up Washington Street and you will see the imposing Neoclassical Courthouse on your right after Cross Street. Designed by the Pain brothers and built by the Deanes in 1835 (or possibly the other way around; sources disagree), it was badly damaged by fire in 1891 and the interior subsequently reconstructed in a busy Early Renaissance style, somewhat at odds with the Neoclassical austerity of the exterior (which, fortunately, survived). A lovely limestone building, the octastyle Corinthian portico is impressive and is surmounted by a sculptural group representing Justice, which was removed for a time but has since been put back. The same cannot be said for the original wrought-iron railings which gave the building (and the street) such a sense of enclosure and are

Courthouse

now sadly lacking. The copper dome is small and can be hard to see from the street; it seems something of an afterthought. Facing the Courthouse across Washington Street is **Courthouse Chambers**, a handsome brick-and-stone commercial building, home to offices and a bar. The building's forceful verticality is neatly balanced by its well-thought-out arched windows, giving it a nice balance, which echoes the Hibernia Buildings on MacCurtain Street (see the MacCurtain Street to City Hall walk). Built in 1874 for the Dwyer family, one of Cork's great merchant clans, it was originally named after them. Washington Street, too, changed its name. Originally called Great George's Street, it was renamed in honour of America's first president in 1918.

••

DID YOU KNOW?

The floor in the old courthouse collapsed during a trial in 1682, forcing the judge to escape through a window.

6 St Francis's

Go up Cross Street and you will see St Francis's ahead of you on Liberty Street. Designed by Alfred Jones and Stephen Kelly in the Byzantine style, this impressive church was built between 1949 and 1953 to replace the more modest Broad Lane Chapel nearby. The Franciscans have been in Cork since the thirteenth century but, like the Augustinians, suffered during the Reformation when they lost their lands. They re-established themselves at Broad Lane, building a small chapel in 1831. A new sacristy was built in 1876 and further improvements were made to the church between 1889 and 1895. The Order also began to acquire property from this time with a view to building themselves a large new church. Like St Augustine's nearby, plans were begun in 1937 but delayed by the Second World War. The church finally opened in 1953. It is in a richly decorated

Byzantine style, with a projecting entrance arcade flanked by square towers topped by octagonal bell towers. The walls are that classic Cork combination of red brick with limestone dressing.

7 St Peter's (former)

Leave St Francis's by turning left onto Liberty Street and then turn left again onto North Main Street. This is a vibrant area, home to Polish and Chinese immigrant communities. The former church of St Peter's will be on the left of the street, facing up Kyle Street. There has been a church here since 1199 and some of Cork's most influential families are buried here. Replaced by the current Gothic-style building in 1788, the church was deconsecrated after 800 years of use in 1949, after which it was used as a storehouse before being renovated into a cultural centre in 1994. Regularly hosting exhibitions, often of photographic work, it is also an interesting place to visit. Built in a light Gothic style, an octagonal belfry sits over the symmetrically placed point-arched doorway to form a tower topped by battlements. The flanking walls are also battlcmented.

St Peter's (former)

ST PETER'S (FORMER)
Opening times: Tuesday – Wednesday, 10 a.m. – 5 p.m., Thursday – Saturday, 10 a.m. – 6 p.m., Sunday and Bank Holidays, 11 a.m. – 3 p.m.
Admission: free

DID YOU KNOW?

A man called Francis Taylor was buried at St Peter's in 1753 but was found next morning sitting on top of his grave with his shroud torn to pieces. He had managed to break out of his coffin and claw his way up through the clay. A man called Joseph Taylor published *The Danger of Premature Internment* in 1816. Might he have been one of the lucky Francis's relations?

8 North Mall

Continue up North Main Street and turn left onto Adelaide Street. Then turn right onto Grattan Street and you will see a type of building known as a **Dutch Billy** across the road at the junction of Henry Street. These were houses built in the Dutch style (note the decorative gables) fashionable after the Dutch Prince of Orange defeated the Catholic James II to claim the throne of England as King William

Dutch Billy, Grattan Street

III in the 1690s. Continue up Grattan Street and you will come to the northern channel of the River Lee at Bachelor's Quay. To your right is **Griffith's Bridge**, a 1960s' replacement for the original Northgate Bridge, an ornate cast-iron structure that was built about

Distillery House with St Vincent's, Sunday's Well

a century earlier. This is also where another of Cork's city gaols was located, built in 1715. The northern counterpart to the Southgate Gaol, both closed down once new prisons were built to the west of the city in the nineteenth century. Keeping the river to your right, walk along Bachelor's Quay and you will come to **St Vincent's Bridge**, a charming pedestrian bridge connecting to North Mall. The first bridge built here was of timber; the present steel structure, with its attractive lattice balustrades, was constructed in 1878. Presiding over North Mall at the end of the bridge is an elegant Georgian mansion. **Distillery House** was another of Cork's breweries, now gone. This three-storey, five-bay house is a particularly handsome example of its kind, while in the background you can catch a glimpse of the artful Gothic massing of St Vincent's in Sunday's Well. **North Mall**, facing the river here, was one of the city's most fashionable addresses in the eighteenth century and home to rich merchants. Built on the site of a Franciscan abbey, some of the houses unearthed coffins when they were being built.

DID YOU KNOW?

King James II attended Mass at the abbey that used to stand where North Mall is today before heading off to lose the Battle of the Boyne in 1690.

9 Mercy Hospital

Return to Bachelor's Quay and follow it as it turns into Grenville Place. The **Lee Maltings** will be across the river to your right. This is one of the most significant industrial complexes in the city. Founded in 1787 as a water-powered flour and corn mill, these magnificent six- and seven-storey buildings were built between 1825 and 1831. A porter brewery also operated here from 1797 to 1813. Porter is a dark beer, also known as stout (like Guinness), made from heavily roasted (or 'malted') barley. Beamish and Crawford bought the brewery in 1813 only to close it down – it was competition. The complex was sold to University College Cork in 1968 and is now home to a number of the university's departments, as well as a sports centre and a theatre. Continue along Grenville Place and you will see the **Mercy Hospital** on your left at the corner of Sheares Street. Originally built as the residence for the Mayor of Cork in 1767, it is in a rather retardataire William and Mary style, with ornately shaped windows. Designed by Davis Ducart, a Sicilian who had come to Ireland to work on the Newry Canal, he also designed Limerick's Custom House. Stuccadore Patrick Osborne did the plasterwork on the staircase, lobby and drawing room, which can still be seen. The Mercy Hospital was founded here by the Sisters of Mercy in 1857, at which time the mayor's office moved to South Mall.

Mercy Hospital

DID YOU KNOW?

Cork has had a mayor since the twelfth century, but the title got upgraded to Lord Mayor in 1900 when the incumbent Daniel J. Hegarty received it from Queen Victoria on her state visit. (The only other city in Ireland to have a Lord Mayor is Dublin.)

Link to University College Cork to Sunday's Well walk: *Continue along Grenville Place and turn right onto Dyke Parade.*

UNIVERSITY COLLEGE CORK TO SUNDAY'S WELL

Approximate walking time: 2 hours and 30 minutes

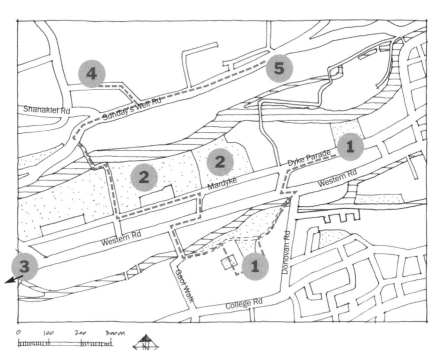

THE WALK: KEY

1 **University College Cork**
2 **Fitzgerald Park**
3 **County Hall**
4 **Cork City Gaol (former)**
5 **St Vincent's**

T HE SUBURBS to the west and north-west of Cork have some important buildings, including the magical University College Cork complex, which has a magnificent quadrangle as well as some architectural masterpieces, such as the Honan Chapel and the Glucksman Gallery. It is also where you can see the old County Gaol. In fact, the walk also leads you past another of Cork's old gaols, the City Gaol, located high in the hills of Sunday's Well, which is where you will find the magnificent church of St Vincent's. Between the university and Sunday's Well you can stroll through the beautifully landscaped Fitzgerald Park, then cross the River Lee via the city's only suspension bridge, from where you can see the imposing bulk of County Hall. The walk begins, however, where the last walk left off, and takes you down Dyke Parade, a pretty residential street that used to be home to university staff and, after a long period of neglect, has now begun to gentrify.

1 University College Cork

Walk along **Dyke Parade**, a pleasant residential street developed from the 1780s onwards. After University College Cork was established in the 1840s it became popular with staff but fell on hard

Dyke Parade

times in the twentieth century, particularly the second half. It has, however, begun to gentrify in recent years which means that some of these lovely old Georgian homes are once again being lived in. Further down the road, on your right-hand side, is the Presentation Brothers school. This was originally based in **Mardyke House**, a fine five-bay, two-storey Georgian home, built as a wedding present around 1812; it was sold to the school in 1922 and is still in magnificent condition, as is **Mardyke Cottage**, next door, a smaller, three-bay Georgian house with exposed sandstone walls. Take the next left and you see the main gates of **University College Cork** ahead of you across Western Road. Founded as one of three Queen's Colleges in Ireland in 1845 (Belfast and Galway were the other two), it became University College Cork in 1908 and was officially renamed National University of Ireland, Cork (NUIC) in 1997 (but the name University College Cork stuck and is the one still used today). The site is appropriate because it is where St Finbarr is thought to have had his famous monastery and school in the seventh century; this is reflected in the university's motto: 'Where Finbarr taught, let Munster learn.' University College Cork officially opened its doors in 1849 and is now home to more than 20,000 students. The main building is by Thomas Deane and Benjamin Woodward. Arranged around three sides of a south-facing quadrangle, known to everyone as the **'Quad'**, this is in a charming English Gothic style reminiscent of Oxford colleges (particularly

DID YOU KNOW?

There is an oak tree in the grounds of University College Cork that was planted by a young First World War soldier, who found it sprouting from an acorn in a friend's pocket after discovering his body in a trench a few days after he died. He brought the sapling here and planted it. It is now a memorial to both of these young men, because he returned to the front and was killed shortly after.

Quad, University College Cork

Magdalen). The north range contains a cloistered walkway which houses Ireland's largest public **collection of Ogham stones**. These are burial or boundary markers that contain the earliest known form of Irish writing. The collection was established in 1861 and the last stone was added in 1945. Most date from the mid fifth to the late seventh centuries. The north range is also home to the **Visitors' Centre** which provides tours, including the George Boole Tour, which tells the story of the university through the eyes of a famous scientist who was Professor of Mathematics here in the nineteenth century. The **Library** and **Aula Maxima** are also housed in this block, which extends to the north out over a wooded precipice which descends to the river.

Other interesting buildings on the campus include the **Crawford Observatory**, completed in 1880 and home to an important collection of telescopes, and the **Lewis Glucksman Gallery**, an award-winning exhibition space by Irish architects O'Donnell and Tuomey from 2004 (see the Architectural Styles chapter for an illustration). Perhaps the most important building of all is the **Honan Chapel** (you can also see an illustration of this in the Architectural Styles chapter). This building is by James McMullen and is built in the Hiberno-Romanesque style. Officially known as St Finbarr's Collegiate Chapel, it is a much-praised example of the Irish Arts and Crafts movement. Built in 1916, and paid for by the Honan family, wealthy Cork merchants, it is modelled on twelfth-century St Cronan's in Roscrea, County Tipperary. The bell tower is inspired by ninth-century round towers. The interior's exquisite mosaic floors are thought to be by German firm of Ludwig Oppenheimer – they are not credited in early guidebooks, probably because of ill feeling towards the Germans after the First World War. The stained-glass windows are magnificent and are by Harry Clarke and the studio of Sarah Purser.

UCC CAMPUS TOURS
Monday – Friday, 3 p.m., Saturday, 12 noon (8 February to 9 December)
Admission charges

GEORGE BOOLE TOURS
Friday, 3 p.m., Saturday, 12 noon (May to September)
Admission charges

LEWIS GLUCKSMAN GALLERY
Opening times: Tuesday – Saturday, 10 a.m. – 5 p.m., Sunday 2 – 5 p.m
Admission: free (donations are welcome)

••

DID YOU KNOW?

The Honan Chapel is railed off from the rest of the University College Cork campus to show it is a house of God, not part of this non-denominational institution.

2 Fitzgerald Park

Leave University College Cork by walking onto Gaol Bridge and you will see the massive gates of the old **Cork County Gaol** on your left facing up it. Built in 1818 to replace the old city-centre prisons, at a time when this area was still in the countryside, the entrance is unusual in that the Greek Doric columns are unfluted. Designed by the Pain brothers, the cell block had three wings and was home to men and women (mostly men), including criminals and those who could not pay their debts. Children as young as six were incarcerated here and public hangings took place out front, a practice deplored by the university, which suspended classes while these happened. Republican prisoners were kept here in 1920 and two of them died on hunger strike, boosting sympathy for the cause of Irish freedom internationally; a plaque by Cork sculptor Seamus Murphy commemorates their sacrifice. The gaol closed in 1946 and was handed over to UCC.

Cross Gaol Bridge and turn right onto Western Road, then take the next left and you will come to the **Mardyke**. This is a continuation of Dyke Parade and takes its name from the dyke, or embankment, constructed here by Edward Webber in 1719. He was descended from Dutch people and so called it *Meer Dyke* (lake dyke) and it quickly became known as 'Mardyke'. Webber owned the marshy land here and decided to drain it, lay out walks and build a red-brick tea house in 1722. It became popular but did not last long after his death in 1735. The park was then bought by James Morrison, Mayor of Cork, who built Dyke House as a private home (it is now the Sacred Heart Missionaries). He also had the grounds professionally landscaped and put in an ornamental pond.

....

DID YOU KNOW?

The Mardyke is mentioned in James Joyce's *A Portrait of the Artist as a Young Man.*

Lord Mayor's Pavilion,
Fitzgerald Park

Right across the Mardyke is the **Cork County Cricket Club**, founded here in 1849, making it the third oldest cricket club in the country (after Phoenix and Trinity Cricket Clubs in Dublin). Its grounds cover about 2.5 hectares (5 acres) and stretch to the river. Next door is **Fitzgerald Park**, Cork's premier public park and one of the city's main visitor attractions. Named after Lord Mayor Edward Fitzgerald, who held the Cork International Exhibition here in 1902/1903, it is beautifully landscaped and contains river walks, a playground, sculptures, a bandstand and a lake. Two buildings are worth seeing: the **Lord Mayor's Pavilion**, a gorgeous Arts and Crafts lodge built for the Exhibition, and the **Cork Public Museum**, a simple two-storey Neoclassical house built by the brewer Charles Beamish in 1845. Originally known as 'The Shrubbery', because of the profusion of planting in its garden, it now houses a fine collection of Irish handcrafts, including silver, glass and lace. It also has archaeological exhibits tracing 7,000 years of human settlement in Cork.

FITZGERALD PARK

Opening times:
November to February: 8.30 a.m. – 5 p.m.
March and October: 8.30 a.m. – 6 p.m.
April and September: 8.30 a.m. – 8 p.m.
May and August: 8.30 a.m. – 9 p.m.
June and July: 8.30 a.m. – 10 p.m.
Saturday, Sunday and Bank Holidays, park opens at 10 a.m.
Admission: free

CORK PUBLIC MUSEUM

Opening times: Monday – Friday, 11 a.m. – 1 p.m., 2.15 – 5 p.m.,
Saturday, 11 a.m. – 1 p.m., 2.15 – 4 p.m., Sunday (April to
September), 3 – 5 p.m.
Admission: free

DID YOU KNOW?

One of the first hot-air balloon trips ever made in Ireland
started from near the Mardyke in 1784 – a journey of nearly
30km (18 miles).

3 County Hall

Leave Fitzgerald Park by Ferry Walk and cross **Daly's Bridge**, one
of the most popular bridges in Cork. Also known as the 'shaky
bridge', it opened in 1927 and is named after James Daly, a
merchant who lived in Sunday's Well and paid for half its cost.
Located at an old ferry crossing, it was designed by Stephen W.
Farrington, a local engineer, and constructed of (mainly) wrought
iron. It is the only suspension bridge in the city and spans about
50m (160 feet). From here you can see, to the left, **County Hall**, a
17-storey office tower built in 1968 on Carrigrohane Road. A
protected structure designed by Cork County Architect Patrick

Cork City Gaol (former)

McSweeney, it got a much-needed facelift between 2002 and 2006 (the original concrete façade was crumbling). Now faced with a more attractive and lighter-looking louvered-glass cladding system, a six-storey extension was added at ground level, and an extra storey on top pushed the tower's height from 64m to 67m (220 feet), making it the tallest building in the country until it was superseded by another Cork landmark, The Elysian, in 2008. The new top floor is home to **Vertigo**, a restaurant with panoramic views of the city and surrounding countryside. **Two Working Men**, a statue by Oisín Kelly, stands outside the complex.

4 Cork City Gaol (former)

Turn right up Sunday's Well Road and take the second left onto Convent Avenue and you will come to Cork City Gaol on your right. A magnificent castle-like structure (complete with battlements), it sits on a south-facing hill in the upmarket suburb of Sunday's Well, so at first glance does not even look like a prison. It was built in 1824 and held males and females who had committed crimes in

Cork city (anyone committing crimes outside the city boundary was held in Cork County Gaol, beside the university). Designed by William Robertson of Kilkenny, it was built by local architect Thomas Deane. The walls are of dark brown sandstone edged with limestone quoins and could accommodate up to 162 men and 48 women in 54 cells. It also had a sick bay and places of worship for both Protestants and Catholics. The governor's office sits at the centre of the complex. A west wing was added in 1870. After 1878, male and female prisoners were separated and this gaol became female-only. (The men were marched over to the County Gaol, while the females were marched here.) Republican prisoners were also held here, including Countess Markievicz in 1919. During the Civil War after Irish independence, the prison was once again home to both males and females. It finally closed down in 1923 but its top floor continued to be used as a radio broadcasting station from 1927 until the 1950s. Most of the rest of the complex fell into decay, however. Fortunately, it was saved from dereliction and turned into a fascinating museum in 1993. Featuring life-size wax figures in furnished cells with sound effects, you can catch a glimpse of how grim life must have been for the unfortunate inmates of a nineteenth-century prison. You can even see some of the prisoners' graffiti on the cell walls. The museum also hosts a permanent exhibition on Ireland's pivotal role in the history of radio. The grounds are beautiful, with many mature trees and a picnic area.

CORK CITY GAOL (FORMER)
Opening times: Daily, 9.30 a.m. – 5 p.m. (April to September);
10 a.m. – 4 p.m. (October to March)
Admission charges

....

DID YOU KNOW?

Famous Irish sculptor John Hogan worked as a draughtsman on some of the drawings for Cork City Gaol.

5 St Vincent's

Return to Sunday's Well Road and turn left and St Vincent's will be on your right after about 150m (500 feet). Built on land donated by local resident Mary MacSwiney, relative of Lord Mayor Terence MacSwiney who died on hunger strike in 1920, this beautiful church is an unmissable landmark on the Cork city skyline. Made of red sandstone with limestone dressing, it was designed by John Benson in a light Gothic style and opened in 1856. The church's interior is by George Goldie, who also added the three-storey **Retreat House** to the west of the church in 1873. This L-shaped block has a delightful point-roofed turret corbelled over a stunted column where the building turns back on itself. The interior of the L forms a lovely little plaza in front of the main entrance of the church. Located on a difficult and steeply sloping site, the church was badly damaged by a storm during construction so plans for a tower and steeple were shelved; pinnacles designed by S.F. Hynes were built instead. Still used as a church, the Retreat House was sold to University College Cork in 2000 and is now their School of Music.

St Vincent's

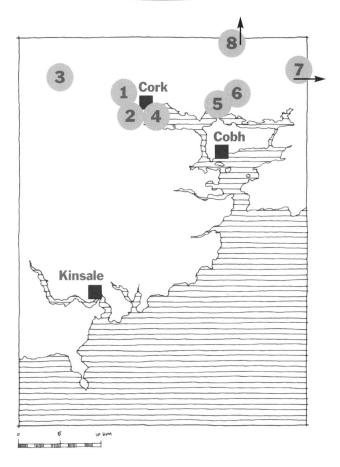

THE WALK: KEY

1 **Old Cork Waterworks**

2 **The Lough**

3 **Blarney Castle**

4 **Blackrock Castle**

5 **Fota House**

6 **Barryscourt Castle**

7 **Ballymaloe House**

8 **Ballyvolane House**

T HIS CHAPTER covers buildings and places of interest that lie outside the city centre, like the Old Cork Waterworks and the Lough. It also covers a number of castles and country houses only a short distance from Cork (in the eastern part of the county) and really worth a visit. This includes picturesque Blackrock Castle, with its Observatory, and Barryscourt Castle, which is only a short distance from Fota House, with its magnificent Arboretum and Wildlife Park. Ballyvolane House and Ballymaloe House are also included, two lovely Irish country houses where it is possible to stay and feel like a friend of the family. Finally, Blarney Castle is included, not only because it is a lovely castle, with stunning grounds, but because it is home to the world-famous Blarney Stone.

1 Old Cork Waterworks

This award-winning heritage centre can be reached by foot from the city centre: simply follow Sunday's Well Road, which turns into Lee Road and you will come to the Waterworks on your left overlooking the river. Lifetime Lab @ Old Cork Waterworks is the best-preserved Victorian pumping station in Ireland. Containing interactive exhibits explaining three centuries of industrial heritage here, these beautiful old buildings command wonderful views of the river. There is also a café. There has been a waterworks here since the 1760s but by the middle of the nineteenth century it had become outdated and was becoming dangerous to the city because the water was getting contaminated by the old reservoirs and pipes. John Benson was

Old Cork Waterworks

commissioned to built a new steam-powered waterworks in 1857, with new reservoirs and cast-iron pipes (to replace wooden ones). The most striking feature of the complex is its magnificent 34m (112-foot) **chimney**. Built in 1858, it not only expelled smoke but was also used to draw air into the boilers to improve combustion. Beautifully decorated in a Lombardo-Romanesque style, each side has blind windows and limestone crosses. The base is that typical Cork combination of grey limestone and red sandstone, as are the **Engine House**, dating from 1863, and the **Turbine House**, from 1888. This is where you can see the three magnificent engines installed between 1905 and 1907 which are, along with the chimney itself, the most striking features of this fascinating complex.

OLD CORK WATERWORKS

Opening times:
Monday – Friday, 9 a.m. – 5 p.m., Saturday, Sunday and Bank Holidays 10 a.m. – 5 p.m. (summer); Monday – Friday, 9 a.m. – 5 p.m. (winter)

Admission charges

2 The Lough

You can get to the Lough, which is located about 2km (1.25 miles) south-west of the city centre, by taking bus 214 to Lough Road. A large shallow lake (only about 1m (3 feet) deep) ringed by a wooded walk, the Lough is popular with anglers as its water is full of pike, carp and other small fish. The water's edge is also home to a wide variety of waterfowl and it is a lovely place to relax. Back when Ireland's winters were colder it was used as a skating rink. It also features in one of Crofton Croker's fairy tales. The fairies allowed a well to be used by local people every morning, provided they remembered to cover it with a stone when they had taken what they needed. One morning a princess forgot to replace the stone and the well flooded over, forming the Lough. The king and all his subjects drowned (including, one presumes, the forgetful princess – although what she was doing fetching water from a well is not made clear by the story).

3 Blarney Castle

Take bus 215 from Cork Bus Station to Blarney village, which is located about 8km (5 miles) north-east of the city. The name Blarney has passed into English as 'smooth flattery'. The power to command such flattery is supposed to be bestowed on anyone who kisses the **Blarney Stone**. Located high in one of the castle parapets, you have to lie on your back and be lowered, head downwards, over the edge of the wall to kiss it, so it is not for the faint-hearted. The current castle, which is a partially restored ruin, was built in 1446 by Dermot MacCarthy, King of Munster and was the third structure built here. A tenth-century wooden hunting lodge was replaced by a stone castle in 1210, which was subsequently demolished, its stones being used for the current castle's foundations. The castle itself is, in fact, only a central keep, all that remains of a much larger fortress. L-shaped, the massive four-storey tower house has a slender tower attached to it topped by battlements with machicolations. Looking like something out of *Game of Thrones*, it was supposedly built by Cormac Láidir (the Strong) MacCarthy of Muskerry in 1446. One of Ireland's most ancient clans, the MacCarthys continued to live here, even managing to hold onto their ancestral home in the face of demands to hand it over to Elizabeth I (see the Note on the Blarney Stone on p. 115). They eventually lost it by being on the wrong side of the English Civil War in the mid-seventeenth century, but when Charles II came to the throne in the Restoration of 1660, they got it back and the head of the family was made Viscount Muskerry and (later) Earl of Clancarty. Donough, the fourth Earl, was brought up as a Protestant in England but converted to Catholicism and supported

THE BLARNEY STONE

The Blarney Stone, famous for its magical power of bestowing eloquence on those who kiss it, was thought to be Jacob's pillow, brought to Ireland by the prophet Jeremiah. It was known as the *Lia Fáil* or 'Fatal Stone' and was used as a throne by Irish kings at Tara. It was then taken to Scotland, presumably in a raid, where it served a similar function for the Scottish kings and was known as the 'Stone of Destiny'. When Cormac MacCarthy, King of Munster, sent 4,000 men to support Robert the Bruce in his fight against the English in 1314, the stone was split in two and half of it brought back as a reward and installed at Blarney Castle. Two centuries later, when the power of the native Irish kings was broken by King Henry VIII, kings and chieftains were converted into earls. This assimilation strategy was continued by Henry's daughter, Elizabeth I, who continued to take over Irish castles and lands. In the case of Blarney, however, Cormac MacDermot MacCarthy, having promised to deliver his castle, kept putting off the Queen by placating her with soft talk, prompting an exasperated Elizabeth to utter: 'Blarney, Blarney, I will hear no more of this Blarney!'

the ill-fated King James II in the early 1690s. Blarney Castle was used as a prison for Protestants in the campaign but when Cork fell to William III in 1690, the Earl of Clancarty was taken prisoner and lost his estates. He died in Hamburg in 1734. The castle then passed through numerous hands before being bought by its current owners, the Jefferyes, in 1703 who, tired of the tourists, built themselves a new mansion elsewhere on the estate. **Blarney House** (also known as Blarney New Castle) was built in 1874 by architect John Lanyon in a Scottish Baronial style. It is not open to the public. The **castle**

grounds consist of a 24-hectare (60-acre) park where the River Martin joins the Blarney River. Beautifully landscaped, they contain a fern garden, a poison garden and a Rock Close thought to have been of importance to druids.

BLARNEY CASTLE

Opening times:

Monday – Saturday

9 a.m. – 5 p.m. (November to February)

9 a.m. – 6 p.m. (March to April and October)

9 a.m. – 6.30 p.m. (May and September)

9 a.m. – 7 p.m. (June to August)

Sundays and Bank Holidays

9 a.m. – 5 p.m. (November to February)

9 a.m. – 6 p.m. (March to October)

Last entry one hour before closing

Admission charges

....

DID YOU KNOW?

There is a legend that the fourth Earl of Clancarty, the last of the MacCarthys to live at Blarney Castle, hid a treasure chest in the lake before going into exile in Germany and that his ghost can still be seen haunting the grounds late at night as he searches for it.

4 Blackrock Castle

Take bus 202 to Blackrock and alight at St Luke's. The castle is a five-minute walk along the River Lee. Officially known as the CIT Blackrock Castle Observatory, this beloved Cork landmark is home to an award-winning interactive astronomy exhibit which highlights recent discoveries in scientific research into the possibility of life in

Blackrock Castle

outer space, as well as a digital planetarium. It is also possible to take tours of the castle, which includes a visit to the dungeons as well as the roof, which has wonderful views of the river and the Tivoli hills beyond. The original castle was built as a defence post in 1582 by the Viceroy of Ireland, Lord Mountjoy, to guard Cork Harbour. The current construction is a fairy-tale fantasy designed by the brothers James and George Pain for Cork Corporation in 1829 and makes excellent use of its picturesque setting. A large round castellated tower, pierced by numerous windows, houses a small banqueting room. A tall slender tower rises above this and has a guidance light for ships on top of it. The central tower is flanked by lower rectangular buildings, and there is a water gate on the river with a flight of steps leading down to the water. There is also the Castle Café on the grounds, which is a lovely place to take a break.

BLACKROCK CASTLE

Opening times:
Monday – Friday, 10 a.m. – 5 p.m.
Saturday and Sunday, 11 a.m. – 5 p.m.

Admission charges
Check the website for opening times, as the castle is sometimes closed for special events.

5 Fota House

Located about 17km (10.5 miles) east of Cork city, Fota can be reached by train. Take the Cork city to Cobh line, alight at Fota Island station and follow the signs to the house, which is a ten-minute walk away. **Fota House** began as a hunting lodge belonging to the aristocratic Smith-Barry family before being substantially remodelled in the 1820s by father-and-son architects Richard and William Morrison. A large austere Regency house, the exterior proportions are strange and somewhat squat, which is probably the result of the architects having to remodel an existing house, although the Doric entrance portico is rather fine when seen close up. It is a pity that the windows do not have their Georgian glazing; the windows now consist of large blank panes, instead of the many smaller window panes typical of the eighteenth century, and this makes the house seem rather dead. The severe Neoclassicism of the house's exterior belies its rich interior, which contains 70 rooms and 60 fireplaces. The elongated entrance hall has lovely yellow scagliola pillars and runs the length of the original house. Owned

Fota House

by University College Cork, the house was lavishly restored in 1999 and opened to the public in 2002. Full of fine paintings and statues, it also contains a pleasant café.

The park, which covers approximately 280 hectares (700 acres), was opened to the public in 1983. The garden around the house is 11 hectares (27 acres) and includes an ornamental pond, a walled Italian garden, and a majestic cedar of Lebanon planted in 1825. There is also a world-famous **Arboretum** established by John Smith-Barry in the 1840s on a reclaimed swamp. It is home to a variety of Asian and American species, including rare shrubs and a number of semi-tropical trees which thrive in Cork's balmy microclimate. It was Smith-Barry's son, Arthur Hugh (with the help of his gardener William Osborne) who really developed the arboretum into the great garden it is today. Fota is also home to a popular **Wildlife Park** with a collection of over 90 species, including tigers, zebras, giraffes, monkeys and kangaroos in its 28 hectares (70 acres). Set up in 1983 as a joint venture between the Zoological Society of Ireland and University College Cork it focuses on breeding and has reintroduced animals to the wild. It also saved the native Irish white-tailed sea eagle from extinction. Feeding times are popular with children, and there is a train linking the different sections of the park, which includes play areas for children, picnic areas and a self-service restaurant.

FOTA HOUSE AND GARDENS

Opening times:

Monday – Saturday, 10 a.m. – 5.30 p.m.

Sunday, 11 a.m. – 5 p.m. (April to September); 11 a.m. – 4 p.m. (October to March)

Last entry one hour before closing

Admission charges

FOTA WILDLIFE PARK

Opening times:

Monday – Saturday, 10 a.m. – 5 p.m.

Sunday, 11 a.m. – 5 p.m.

Admission charges

THE CURSE OF THE BARRYMORES

Arthur Hugh Smith-Barry was created Lord Barrymore in 1902, reviving the old family title. He married Lady Mary Wyndham-Quin but their son was cursed by a local girl who had been hired to act as a wet nurse (until an Englishwoman arrived – the boy had been born prematurely). When the Irish girl was dismissed she was furious and swore that henceforth no male would ever inherit the estate. The baby died within a year and the house eventually passed to their daughter, Dorothy Bell, who died in 1976, after which Fota was bought by University College Cork.

6 Barryscourt Castle

The best way to get to Barryscourt Castle is by car. It is located in Carrigtwohill, just off the N25 about 20km (12.5 miles) east of Cork. This atmospheric tower house was the ancestral home of the Barry family, Earls of Barrymore (whose descendants, the Smith-Barrys, built nearby Fota House). The Barrys were descended from the de Barry family who established themselves in this part of Ireland in the twelfth century. One of the great Anglo-Norman families, with numerous branches, the most powerful, the Barrymores (from the Irish *Barra mór* or 'Great Barry') had their home in Barryscourt. This line died out in 1556 and Barryscourt passed to a cousin, James FitzRichard of the Barryroes (*Barra rua* or 'Red Barry'). The present castle is thought to date to the 1550s, based on its architectural style. The family supported the Desmond Rebellions of 1569 and 1579 and severely damaged their own castles to prevent them falling into English hands (Barryscourt itself was threatened by an army led by Sir Walter Raleigh). Pardoned by Elizabeth I, the family repaired Barryscourt. The castle consisted of a tower house with smaller outer buildings ranged around a courtyard protected by a bawn and

Barryscourt Castle

Further Afield

curtain wall, which was typical of castles in sixteenth-century Ireland. Turrets project from the top of three of the tower's corners, while the ruins of what was probably a large dining hall stand next to it. There is also a dungeon into which prisoners were dropped down from above. Barryscourt ceased to be the Barry family's main residence in 1617 but it was still important enough to be captured by government forces during the Irish Confederate War in 1645 and you can still see cannonball marks on some of the walls. The castle then fell into disuse. An important local family of landowners, the Coppingers, built a house next to it in the early eighteenth century, but this has since disappeared. The Barryscourt Trust was set up in 1987 to conserve and develop the castle, which was reroofed in the 1990s. It is currently closed for further repairs.

BARRYSCOURT CASTLE
Currently closed

7 Ballymaloe House

The best way to get to Ballymaloe House is by car. Take the N25 to Shanagarry, near Midleton. The house is located about 30km (18.5 miles) east of Cork. Ballymaloe is a charming, rambling Georgian guest house which sits on a 300-acre farm and has lovely gardens, a tennis court and a (summer) swimming pool, as well as croquet lawn. It is also home to the world-famous **Ballymaloe Cookery School** run by the Allen family. There is also the **Ballymaloe Grainstore**, a converted seventeenth-century farm building now used as a conference venue that hosts cultural events.

The Allen family moved to Ballymaloe just after the Second World War. The farm provided fresh produce while the nearby river and sea provided excellent fish and shellfish. Myrtle Allen decided to open a restaurant in 1964, The Yeats Room, which was hung with pictures by Jack Yeats, and three years later opened some of the bedrooms to paying guests. Success led to the founding of a cookery school, which has since garnered an international reputation. The house itself is interesting, and very Irish. It began life as a castle for the FitzGeralds of Imokilly in the sixteenth century and was enlarged in 1602 by Sir John FitzEdmund FitzGerald. It now looks predominantly early eighteenth-century, with some of the windows still having the thick glazing bars typical of the time. It consists of a simple two-storey six-bay block with one of the original castle towers at one end. There is also a three-storey gable-ended range at right angles to the main block, forming an L. The interiors have simple Adamesque decoration. Confiscated by Cromwell in the mid seventeenth century, after the Restoration in 1660 it was occupied by William Penn (see *Did You Know?* below). It then passed through quite a number of hands, including Hugh Lumley, who added some new buildings. Then it had more owners until finally being bought by the Allens in 1947, who have stayed here ever since. It is a lovely house, with wonderful food, and makes for a great place to stay.

• •

DID YOU KNOW?

William Penn, the man who founded the US state of Pennsylvania, lived at Ballymaloe House in the seventeenth century. He used it as a base to manage his father's nearby estate at Shanagarry.

Ballymaloe House

Further Afield

123

8 Ballyvolane House

Ballyvolane House

The best way to get to Ballyvolane House is by car. Take the M8 to Castlelyons, near Fermoy. The house is located about 35km (22 miles) north of the city and is a warm, welcoming family home surrounded by woods, fields and a lovely garden. You can play tennis, badminton or croquet and there are trout lakes and private salmon fishing on the River Blackwater nearby. The food is simple, delicious home-cooked fare with ingredients from the walled garden or sourced from local artisan producers. There is also the famous home-made Bertha's Revenge Gin. The house was originally built by Sir Richard Pyne in 1728 (replacing an earlier medieval mansion belonging to the Coppingers). It received a Victorian Italianate makeover in 1847, when the top floor was removed and a pitched roof was placed over a heavy cornice. The windows also lost their Georgian glazing. The Green family bought it in 1953 and their descendants still live here today and operate it as a guest house. The interior is remarkably lovely. The large hall has a screen of slender Corinthian marbleised columns and is thought to be by the same architect who designed Cashel Palace, County Tipperary. A fine staircase leads to well-proportioned bedrooms which have wonderful views over the meticulously maintained grounds.

• •

DID YOU KNOW?

Many of the magnificent trees on the Ballyvolane estate were planted by Thomas Pennefeather, a cousin of the Pynes, who came to stay for a fortnight but remained for 40 years, acting as agent for the estate.

COBH

Approximate walking time: 3 hours

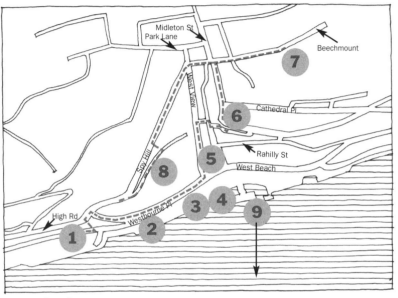

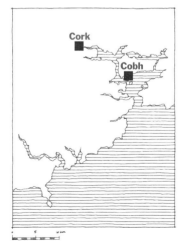

THE WALK: KEY

1 **Cobh Heritage Centre**

2 **Sirius Arts Centre**

3 **Waterfront**

4 **Titanic Experience**

5 **Casement Square**

6 **St Colman's Cathedral**

7 **St Benedict's Priory**

8 **The Crescent**

9 **Spike Island**

COBH (PRONOUNCED 'COVE') is a pretty seaside town about 23km (14.5 miles) from Cork and easily reached by train. Located on the south coast of Great Island (one of six islands in Cork Harbour – and now linked to the mainland by a causeway), its colourful Victorian seafront and steeply stepped terraces command wonderful views of one of the world's finest natural harbours. Until around 1800 Cobh was a small fishing village but with the Napoleonic Wars (1803–1815) Cork Harbour turned into an important refuelling and assembly point for the British navy. By the time Queen Victoria visited in 1849 the village had turned into a busy town and was renamed Queenstown in her honour (it reverted to its original name on Ireland's independence in 1922). Thanks to its strategic location on the busy transatlantic route Cobh became a major port, especially for passenger liners. The *Sirius* made the first steam-powered Atlantic crossing from here in 1838, and Cobh was the last place the *Titanic* made landfall before setting off on its doomed maiden voyage in 1912 (you can learn more about this at the Titanic Experience). Today, Cobh is still a major port of call for luxury cruise ships but it also has a sadder history in passenger transport because it was from here that many Irish emigrants caught their last glimpse of home before emigrating to America or Canada, or being transported as convicts to Australia. (Between 1848 and 1950 over 2.5 million Irish men, women and children left Cobh, making it the largest port for emigration in the country – the Cobh Heritage Centre has poignant exhibitions on this).

Cobh is unusual in that it embraces the sea (most Irish seaside towns tend to turn their back to it). It also has an almost

Italian feel (at least on a sunny day), thanks to its colourful Victorian Neoclassical buildings. The waterfront has a promenade and is graced by some lovely buildings, including the Sirius Arts Centre (originally a yacht club). It also contains two rather fine squares. Casement Square contains a memorial to the *Lusitania*, which sank off Kinsale Head in 1915 after being torpedoed by the Germans, and the old Town Hall and Market Building, which is not only home to the Tourist Information Office but contains a triumphal arch, unusual in Ireland, under which a road leads up to West View, a steeply sloped street known locally as 'the pack of cards' and probably the most photographed street in the country.

Presiding majestically over all of this is the magnificent Gothic Revival St Colman's Cathedral, while beyond this lies one of the town's most delightful buildings, St Benedict's Priory; originally the Admiralty, it has a double row of verandas overlooking the harbour, from where you can see the fine old naval complex on Haulbowline Island and, further away, the old fortress and prison complex on Spike Island, named as Europe's Leading Tourist Attraction at the World Travel Awards in 2017. Finally, there is a magnificent curved terrace known as The Crescent, which will lead you back to where the walk started.

For anyone with small children, or those unable to tackle the town's steep streets, a good way of getting around is to hop on the Cobh Road Train which makes hourly tours of the main sites, including the Titanic Memorial Garden located on the eastern edge of town.

1 Cobh Heritage Centre

The Cobh Heritage Centre is attached to the town's beautifully restored Victorian railway station (which also features a maritime exhibition on its platform). At the Heritage Centre you can see The Queenstown Story, a multimedia exhibition outlining the town's origins and history, including the informative and emotive story of Irish emigration – this also includes involuntary transportation of convicts to Australia up to 1867. You can also learn about Cobh's connection with more luxurious transatlantic passenger traffic, such as the *Titanic* (Cobh was the doomed liner's last port of call in 1912) and the *Lusitania* (which sank off Kinsale Head after being torpedoed by a German submarine in 1915 – the old Market Building on Casement Square was used as a mortuary). The centre also offers a **Genealogical Family History Research Profile** service designed to allow anyone, even if they have no knowledge of how to go about conducting genealogical research, to obtain detailed custom-made analysis of all Irish records relevant to a particular ancestor. There is a charge for a one-hour session with a trained genealogist, and it is advisable to book in advance. Just outside the station on the seafront stands the **statue of Annie Moore**, who passed through US immigration at Ellis Island, New York on 1 January 1892. As the first person processed at the new facility she was awarded a $10 gold coin. She went on to marry the son of German Catholic immigrants who worked at Manhattan's Fulton Fish Market. Together they had eleven children. She died on 6 December 1924 and is buried in the Calvary Cemetery, Queens, New York. Her unmarked grave was only identified in 2006 and is now graced by a Celtic Cross of Irish limestone. Head across Westbourne Place and climb the steps to High Road and you will see the **Cobh Museum** in a former Scots Presbyterian church across the road. This pretty little building, with its miniature spire, dates from the 1850s and is home to a small museum that showcases the history of Cobh, and Great Island, in a series of changing exhibitions that feature old watercolours and photographs of the town as well as some intricate models of ships.

COBH HERITAGE CENTRE

Opening times: Monday – Saturday, 9.30 a.m. – 5.30 p.m., Sundays and Bank Holidays, 11 am – 5.30 p.m. (April to October); Monday – Saturday, 9.30 a.m. – 4.30 p.m., Sundays and Bank Holidays, 11 a.m. – 4.30 p.m. (November to March)

Admission charges

COBH MUSEUM

Opening times: Daily, 9.30 a.m. – 6 p.m. (April to October); 9.30 a.m. – 5 p.m. (November to March), last admission one hour before closing

Admission charges

....

DID YOU KNOW?

Between 1848 and 1950 more than 6 million people emigrated from Ireland, 2.5 million of them from Cobh.

2 Sirius Arts Centre

Walk down Westbourne Place and you will see the Sirius Arts Centre on your right overlooking the water. This Italianate gem of a building was built in 1854 as the Royal Cork Yacht Club, thought to be the oldest in the world. Originally founded on Haulbowline Island in 1720, it moved to Crosshaven (for better moorings) in 1969. Funds for the building were originally provided by James Smith-Barry of Fota House, so it was he who got to select the architect. Anthony Salvin was better known for his vast Gothic country houses and work on Windsor Castle and the Tower of

Haulbowline Island

London; this was his first (and only) commission in Ireland. Budget constraints may have had a hand in the simple yet light-hearted style of the building, which is graced by a triple-arched loggia overlooking the water (a detail subtly repeated and varied on each façade). The building was sold to University College Cork in 1969 but plans to establish a marine research centre fell through and it became derelict. Then, in 1988 a group of local people clubbed together to buy and restore it. The Sirius Arts Centre, named after the first steam-powered ship to cross the Atlantic from Cobh in 1838, is a multidisciplinary arts organisation which hosts a varied programme of events including art exhibitions, musical recitals and even has an artist's residency. It opened in 1995, giving a vibrant new lease of life to this lovely little building.

SIRIUS ARTS CENTRE
Opening times: Tuesday – Friday, 10.30 a.m. – 5 p.m.,
Saturday and Sunday, 1 to 5 p.m.
Admission: free

3 Waterfront

Continue along Westbourne Place. This is Cobh's elegant waterfront and overlooks the **Promenade**, with its park, playground and bandstand. The rather fine terrace of Neoclassical buildings on your left was designed by Decimus Burton in 1849. It was never fully completed but has had a strong influence on the rest of the town's stylistic development. The terrace begins with a **Methodist church**, now closed (it was, for a time, a nightclub) in a lovely warm sandstone. This has a tall Corinthian portico topped by a pepper-pot cupola. Thought to have been designed by Burton himself, there is no evidence to support this (although no one actually knows who the architect of this fine building is). Continue along the terrace and you will come to the **Commodore Hotel**. Built as the Queen's Hotel, this is Irish Neoclassicism with a distinctly Italian accent and the exterior is probably the finest on the whole terrace, the rest of which is speculative property development. Further along the terrace, where it curves into Casement Square, is the Gothic **Bank of Ireland**, and there are also some lovely original shopfronts.

4 Titanic Experience

Located on the waterfront at the end of the promenade facing onto Casement Square sits the former White Star Line Office. This symmetrical single-storey building was the shipping company's ticket office and led to their pier, from which the last 123 passengers boarded the ill-fated *Titanic* on 11 April 1912. The **Titanic Experience** is an exhibition full of fascinating facts about the famous liner's sinking. It is also possible to catch a glimpse of what life was like for those on board, from the richest in first class to the poor emigrants in steerage. For anyone interested in knowing more about this disaster there is also **The Titanic Trail**, a guided walking tour that brings to life the maritime, military and emigrant history of Cobh and Cork Harbour. Informative and fun, you actually visit places such as piers, buildings and streets that the liner's last passengers would have used. And as if that were not enough, there is also a **Titanic Memorial Garden** located at the eastern edge of the town. This peaceful little park, which features a glass wall inscribed with the names of the last passengers who boarded at Cobh, can be reached on foot. Simply follow Harbour Row, which turns into Connolly Road and then onto The Mall. Alternatively, you could hop on the **Cobh Road Train** which makes hourly tours of the main tourist spots, including this garden.

TITANIC EXPERIENCE

Opening times: Daily, 10 a.m. – 5.30 p.m. (January to April and October to December), last tour 4.45 p.m.; 9 a.m. – 6 p.m. (May to September), last tour 5.15 p.m.

Admission charges

THE TITANIC TRAIL

Walks last 45–60 minutes and depart from the Commodore Hotel daily at 11 a.m. (with an extra walk at 2 p.m. from June to August) (booking is recommended)

Admission charges

5 Casement Square

Casement Square is named after the Irish human rights campaigner Roger Casement, who was martyred for the cause of Irish freedom – executed for treason by the British in 1916. At the centre of the square stands the **Lusitania Memorial**, sculpted by Jerome Connor to commemorate those who lost their lives when the passenger liner was sunk off Kinsale Head in 1915. Torpedoed by a German submarine, it sank within sight of land. Survivors and bodies of the dead were brought to Cobh where a memorial service has been held every year for the 1,198 people who lost their lives. Memorial glass headstones mark the graves of the 145 who are buried in the Old Church Cemetery just outside the town. The memorial is somewhat stark, as befits its theme. It sits at the centre of a shallow flight of semicircular steps with a semicircular stone

THE *TITANIC*

Built in Belfast, and supposedly unsinkable, the *Titanic* hit an iceberg on its maiden voyage to New York and sank on 15 April 1912 with appalling loss of life. The largest ship in the world at the time, it was the second in a series of three luxurious ocean liners operated by the White Star Line and built by Harland and Wolff. Her designer, Thomas Andrews, died in the disaster. The ship's name was a byword for luxury and technological prowess, but it was this prowess that probably led to disaster – if the ship had not been trying so hard to win the Blue Riband (for the fastest transatlantic crossing) it may have had more time to avoid the fatal iceberg. The disaster was compounded by the fact that the *Titanic* was carrying far too few lifeboats (even though the number exceeded official requirements at the time, which were based on weight, not passenger numbers). Of the estimated 2,224 passengers and crew on board, more than 1,500 died, making it one of the worst peacetime maritime disasters in history. Public inquiries in Britain and the United States led to improvements in maritime safety, and the establishment of the International Convention for the Safety of Life at Sea (SOLAS), which still governs maritime traffic today. The wreck of the *Titanic* was discovered in 1985 lying at a depth of 3,784m (12,415 feet) on the North Atlantic seabed. Cobh was the ship's last landfall, and was where the liner's final 123 passengers went on board.

Casement Square

ROGER CASEMENT

Roger Casement (1864–1916) was born in Dublin and worked
for the British Foreign Office as a diplomat before becoming a
humanitarian activist and Irish nationalist (he was also a poet
of some renown). Knighted in 1911, he was stripped of his
honours before being executed for treason in 1916. It was his
1905 report on the abuses in the Belgian Congo that earned
him his reputation as the father of human rights. His
investigations gave him a profound distrust of imperialism,
which led to his efforts to enlist German help for Ireland's
1916 Easter Rising. He was caught and convicted of treason.
Before his trial, in an effort to discredit him, the British
government circulated excerpts of what were supposed to be
his private diaries which contained lurid details about his
homosexual activities (considered a criminal offence at the
time), a cynical move calculated to erode support in an era of
social conservatism (debate has raged ever since about the
authenticity of these diaries). Casement was executed in
Pentonville Prison, London, on 3 August 1916.

bench behind. A rather sinister-looking angel stands atop a plinth in front of which stand two men, one with head bowed, the other looking defiant, despite having hands crossed somewhat submissively at the wrists. Behind the memorial you can see the elegantly symmetrical former **Town Hall and Market Building** which houses the **Tourist Information Office** (on the ground floor on the left-hand side, with access beyond the archways). This two-storey Neoclassical structure has thirteen bays, the central three of which protrude slightly under a pediment over the three arches through which the road runs uphill. Thought to be designed by Alexander Deane, it opened in 1852 and had a variety of functions, including market, courthouse and tax collection point. It was also used as a temporary mortuary for the victims of the *Lusitania* in 1915.

6 St Colman's Cathedral

Go through the arch under the old Town Hall and Market Building and you will be on **West View**, a steeply sloping Victorian street whose terrace of colourfully painted gabled houses on the

West View

right-hand side still has most of its original bay windows. Known locally as 'the pack of cards', this has to rank as one of the most picturesque (certainly one of the most photographed) streets in Ireland. Turn right across the small car park to Lower Midleton Street, then right again and immediately take a left and climb the steps to Cathedral Place. Cross this sloping street and take the next set of steps which will lead you up to **St Colman's Cathedral** perched high above the town. This Gothic Revival masterpiece, by Edward Pugin and George Ashlin, was their most important commission; they won it in 1867 (the year Ashlin married Pugin's sister Mary). It was consecrated in 1919. The spire is 90m (300 feet), one of the tallest in the country, and echoes the architects' Augustinian church in Dublin, although it does not have the more forceful wedge-shape of that earlier tower. (There is, however, a reduced wedge-shaped tower terminating the north aisle here.) The original design for the cathedral was

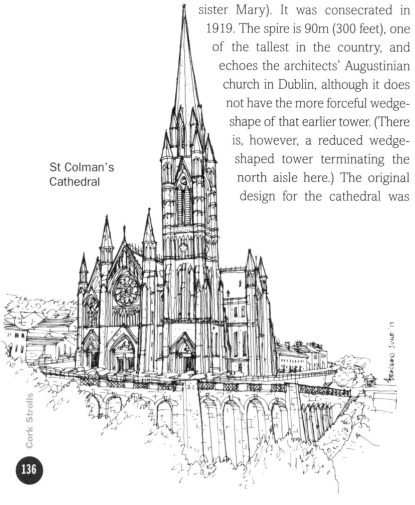

St Colman's
Cathedral

ST COLMAN

St Colman (530–606) was a monk who founded a monastery at Cloyne in County Cork in the sixth century. He was also one of the earliest poets to write in the Irish language. Some of his poems survive, including a panegyric on Saint Brendan. It is not known if he was brought up a Christian. His first training was as a poet (also known as a bard or *file* – this specialist education could take up to twelve years). St Colman went on to St Iarlaithe's school in Tuam and became a preacher in County Cork, which was still heathen at the time. He died in 606, and 24 November is now his feast day.

twice revised and the tower moved to its southern location, at the most dominant position above the town, giving it an almost talismanic status, as it was the last thing many emigrants saw as they departed Ireland forever. The building's hillside site required elaborate foundations and these feature impressive arcades that form a dramatic embankment (which pushed up the costs). The exterior is a lovely blueish-grey Dalkey granite, brought by sea to Cobh. The interior is impressive and beautiful, with the nave's arcades, triforia and clerestories all echoing Ss Peter and Paul's church in Cork, also by the same architects. The cathedral was in use by 1879, but it was only in 1893 that the Bath stone cladding was added, allowing for the amazing carving that so enriches its interior, something that is further enhanced by the stained glass. The exterior carving is also very fine, and features a surprising number of demons as well as the 2.4m (8 foot) Carrara marble statue of St Colman over the west entrance by Dublin sculptor Joseph O'Reilly. The clock is by Smith of Derby (who also made the carillon) and its movement is one of the largest in Ireland. It has three faces, each 2.3m (7.5 ft) in diameter and has Westminster chimes (where four bells chime out the quarter hours). The cathedral survived the twentieth century without being ravaged by the demands of Vatican II and so remains the only Catholic Victorian cathedral in the country which still has its interior intact.

7 St Benedict's Priory

Leave St Colman's Cathedral by turning right, and walk up Sandymount. Turn right onto John O'Connell Street and you will come to the gates of St Benedict's Priory just where the street veers to the left onto Beechmount. You will see a little gate lodge to the right of the gates. Walk up the drive where there is a monastic heritage centre that has an exhibition on the history of monasticism in Ireland. The building itself was built as **Admiralty House** for the British Navy in the 1880s and has the unusual but beautiful feature of the double tiers of verandas facing the sea. The United States used it as their naval base when they joined the First World War in 1917, and the last admiral's visitors' book is on display. Now home to Benedictine nuns, the chapel, Bible Garden and tearooms are all open to the public. The Bible Garden covers about 0.6 of a hectare (1.5 acres) and is laid out in the form of a Jerusalem Cross (which means that all four strokes of the cross are of equal length, unlike the Christian cross, where one is longer). Beautifully planted with mature trees, it is a peaceful place to stroll and has breathtaking views of Cobh and Cork Harbour.

8 The Crescent

Retrace your steps down John O'Connell Street and you will come to Canon O'Leary Place. Turn right onto Midleton Street and you will be in the part of town known as the **Top of the Hill**, famous for its restaurants and pubs. Turn left off Midleton Street onto Park Lane and then take a left onto Park View and you will see West View again, this time from the top. Then take a right onto Spy Hill and go downhill and you will pass the impressive seven-bay bulk of the **Bishop's Palace** on your left. This large plain two-storey-over-basement house was built around 1860 and is in good condition. The portico has Doric pilasters and columns. Just after its gates you will see a winding set of steps. Go down them and you will come to **The Crescent**, a lovely street and one of Ireland's urban delights. This terrace of thirteen mid-nineteenth-century Neoclassical houses is arranged in a gentle curve. If you go to the left and walk to the end you will enjoy one of the most spectacular views of St Colman's

The Crescent

Cathedral. Then retrace your steps and follow the curve all the way to the end and you will see a set of gates on your left. These lead into a beautifully landscaped park nestling under the houses, the perfect place to see The Crescent in all its glory. The terrace is remarkably intact, probably because the houses rarely change hands, most being handed down through the generations. Wander the park at will, then head back out onto The Crescent and turn left. It soon joins Spy Hill. Continue downhill and you will find yourself back at the Cobh Museum.

9 Spike Island

Spike Island is one of six islands situated in Cork Harbour and can be reached by ferry from Kennedy Pier in the centre of Cobh. Covering 42 hectares (104 acres), a monastery was established here in the sixth century and it later became a British army base. A number of forts were built here, including one begun in 1804 but left incomplete at the end of the Napoleonic War eleven years later. The 10-hectare (24-acre) Fort Mitchel was completed around 1850. Originally called Fort Westmoreland, it was renamed Fort Mitchel after the Irish Nationalist hero held prisoner here in the 1840s. Designed by General Vallency, it was large enough to garrison 3,000 men, making it one of the largest fortresses of its type in the world. It also represented cutting-edge military technology at the time. Known as a bastion or star-shaped fort, the star's points defend any part of the island as well as the fortress itself. More used as a prison than a fortress throughout its history, as many as 2,300 inmates were crammed into its small cells in the nineteenth century and it has the dubious reputation of being the largest ever prison in either Ireland or the United Kingdom. It was from here that thousands of convicts were shipped to the penal colony of Australia. Recently renovated, it is now possible to visit the cells, and there are interactive displays showing what life was like for prisoners from the Victorian era to the present day. There is also a gun park with an impressive display of artillery. Guided tours are available, including an after-dark tour, or you can simply walk around the island to enjoy lovely views of the harbour. There is also a café and some picnic areas.

SPIKE ISLAND FERRIES

Saturday and Sunday, 12 noon and 2 p.m. (March, April and September)
Daily, 12 noon and 2 p.m. (May and September)
Hourly sailings daily, 11 a.m. – 3 p.m. (June)
Hourly sailings daily, 10 a.m. – 3 p.m. (July and August)
Check website for details of November sailings

Admissions charges

• •

DID YOU KNOW?

The man who designed Fort Mitchel, General Vallency, was rather unusual in that he had four wives (although not at the same time) and fourteen children.

KINSALE

Approximate walking time: 6 hours

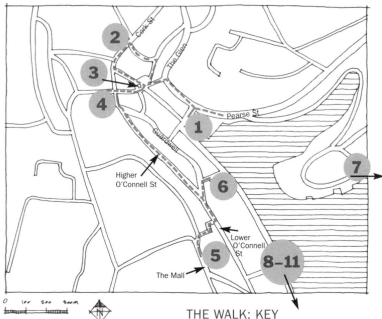

Cork St

The Glen

Pearse St

Guardwall

Higher
O'Connell St

Lower
O'Connell
St

The Mall

0   100   200   300m

N

THE WALK: KEY

1 **Kinsale Tourist Office**
2 **Desmond Castle**
3 **Kinsale Regional Museum**
4 **St Multose**
5 **Municipal Hall**
6 **Kinsale Harbour**
7 **Charles Fort**
8 **James Fort**
9 **9/11 Garden of Remembrance**
10 **Lusitania Museum**
11 **Old Head of Kinsale**

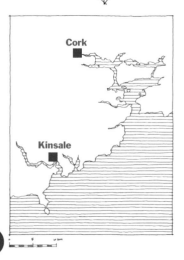

Cork

Kinsale

L OCATED only about 28km (17 miles) south of Cork, the picturesque seaside town of Kinsale nestles within gently rolling hills on the estuary of the Bandon River and has a breathtakingly beautiful natural harbour lined by a long V-shaped waterfront. You can get here by taking bus 226 from Cork, either from Parnell Place or Kent Train Station. Kinsale takes its name from the Irish *Ceann tSáile*, meaning Head of the Sea, and marks the start (or end, depending on your direction of travel) of the stunning Wild Atlantic Way, a 2,750km (1,700-mile) trail that takes you up Ireland's west coast, and the longest such coastal route in the world.

Kinsale may seem like a sleepy little town today, but it is steeped in history. Once one of the most important ports in the country, it was also the scene of the famous Battle of Kinsale in 1601, which saw the power of the native Irish chieftains finally broken by the English, despite help from the Spanish. The great northern clan leaders O'Neill and O'Donnell were defeated after a 100-day siege of the town and fled to the continent, an event now known as the Flight of the Earls. This left the English free to redistribute Irish land to lords more loyal and signalled the end of the Gaelic way of life, a devastating blow to Irish heritage, language and culture, and something the country never really recovered from. Kinsale developed into an important shipbuilding town in the seventeenth century, and up to about 1800 it was the only port in Ireland where British navy ships could be refitted. Kinsale itself had a fleet of 50 or so ships while merchants from the West Indies and America would often put in here. Early in the eighteenth century Alexander Selkirk set sail from Kinsale on a voyage that saw him stranded on a Pacific island, inspiring Daniel Defoe to write *Robinson Crusoe*. In the twentieth century the town entered a decline, but this was halted later in the century when it became a popular holiday destination, especially for recreational sailing and deep-sea fishing. The Kinsale Regatta takes place annually on the first weekend in August. The town also established itself as Ireland's gourmet capital, with excellent restaurants, many of them specialising in fish and seafood. The Kinsale Gourmet Festival is held every October.

The town itself is pretty, with narrow winding streets, some of them stepped, and colourfully painted shops and houses overlooking the busy harbour. Compass Hill behind the town has wonderful sea views. The Kinsale Regional Museum is housed in the seventeenth-century Dutch-style courthouse. This sits close to the 800-year-old St Multose church and the Desmond Castle (which was built round 1500). There is also a charming castle-like Municipal Hall, and two wonderful seventeenth-century forts, Charles Fort and James Fort, guarding the estuary and only a short distance from the town by foot. Finally, you can visit the moving 9/11 Garden of Remembrance and the nearby Lusitania Museum, both of which commemorate the loss of innocent lives, and the Old Head of Kinsale, which has wonderful views of the Atlantic Ocean.

1 Kinsale Tourist Office

Located at the corner of Pier Road and Cork Street, the Kinsale Tourist Office is a good place to get information on the town and its various attractions. This is also where you can get information on the various walks you can do here, including **Dermot Ryan's Kinsale Heritage Town Walks** and **Don and Barry's Historic Stroll**, which give an idea of what life was like in Kinsale from the time it was a medieval walled town up to the sinking of the *Lusitania* in 1915. You can also follow **Kinsale Ghost Tours**, a tour with a difference run by two local actors. It starts and ends at The Tap Tavern, weaving its way through back streets, and features spooky surprises and stories throughout.

Kinsale Harbour
(from Summercove)

DERMOT RYAN'S KINSALE HERITAGE TOWN WALKS
Opening times: Daily, 1.30 a.m. – 12 noon, 4.30 – 6 p.m.
Admission charges

DON AND BARRY'S HISTORIC STROLL
Opening times: Daily, from 11.15 a.m.
Admission charges

KINSALE GHOST TOURS
Opening times: Daily, 9 p.m. (summers)
Admission charges

2 Desmond Castle

Leave the Kinsale Tourist Office by turning right onto Emmet Place, then take another right onto Long Quay and you will see **Perryville**, a charming Victorian townhouse which is now a boutique hotel, on your left overlooking the harbour. Originally two Georgian houses, these were remodelled into one in the 1890s by Captain Adam Warren-Perry. The junction is masked by the three-storey bay which was added in the middle. The ground floor has elaborate Moorish plasterwork over its entrance archway, and this is overhung by an elaborate cast-iron veranda opening off the first floor. All is in mint condition. Retrace your steps up Long Quay, which turns into **Pearse Street**, a busy shopping street with a variety of architectural styles, predominantly Victorian. Then take a left onto Market Street and turn right up **Newman's Mall**, a lively little laneway full of tables from neighbouring eateries. Follow Newman's Mall as it veers to the right, then take a left up Chairman's Lane and you will see the **Desmond Castle** at the top of the street on Cork Street. Also known as the French Prison, this rare example of an Irish urban tower house was built around 1500 as the custom house. It had storehouses to the rear and offices on the first and second floors, where there was also a residence. It may seem a little out of town now but actually the castle's upper

Desmond Castle

floors command excellent views of Kinsale and it was built next to the Cork gate in the old city wall, making it one of the most strategic spots in the town. Built by Maurice Bacach (the lame) FitzGerald, you can see his family coat of arms over the door. The tenth Earl of Desmond, he was descended from an important Anglo-Norman family which invaded Ireland in the twelfth century. These families gradually became assimilated into the Irish way of life, becoming 'more Irish than the Irish themselves'. They followed traditional Gaelic customs, including the speaking of Irish. Kinsale had originally been granted to Milo de Cogan by Henry II in the twelfth century but after centuries of fighting with the MacCarthys (of Blarney Castle), Desmond offered the town protection – in exchange for customs revenue (Kinsale was one of Ireland's most important ports at the time). The townspeople gladly accepted and the castle was built around 1500. During the Battle of Kinsale in 1601 the Spanish used it to store arms, then during the eighteenth century it was used to house prisoners of war, mostly Spanish and French, hence the local nickname French Prison. During the Great Famine in the 1840s it became a workhouse. It was declared a National Monument in 1938 and was restored. It was restored again in the 1960s and, most recently, between 1986 and 1992. It is now home to the **International Museum of Wine**, which features a permanent exhibition on Ireland's involvement with the wine industry worldwide. Many wealthy Irish Catholic families left Ireland in the eighteenth century, establishing themselves in France, Spain and Italy, and famous vineyards like Phelan, Barton and Hennessy are all descended from these Wild Geese (now known as the 'Wine Geese').

DESMOND CASTLE / INTERNATIONAL MUSEUM OF WINE
Opening times: Daily, 10 a.m. – 6 p.m.
Admission charges

• •

DID YOU KNOW?

The fifteenth Earl of Desmond rebelled (unsuccessfully) against Elizabeth I in the 1580s. He was executed and his family lost their lands (vast tracts of Cork, Kerry and Waterford). These were then granted to a syndicate headed by the explorer Sir Walter Raleigh.

3 Kinsale Regional Museum

Leave Desmond Castle by turning right onto Cork Street, then take a left onto Market Lane and you will see the Kinsale Regional Museum on your right after Market Place, which is where the town's fish shambles used to be located. This Dutch-style building, with its three slate-covered gables, is also known as the Market House and was built in 1600; a new frontage was added in 1706. It was for many years Kinsale's courthouse. Now home to the Kinsale Regional Museum, it displays an eclectic collection of items relating to the town's maritime and military history. This includes maps, models and letters which paint a fascinating picture of what life in Kinsale was like in centuries gone by. There is a **bronze scale model** of the town as it would have looked in 1601 in front of the museum. One of four walled towns in County Cork in the fourteenth century, construction started on Kinsale's walls in 1380 and the town had five gates. Besieged in 1601, Kinsale was captured after the Battle of the Boyne in 1690 and had its walls demolished (although there was still a gate standing as late as 1805).

Kinsale Regional
Museum

DID YOU KNOW?

The inquest into the sinking of the *Lusitania* took place in the panelled courtroom upstairs in the Kinsale Regional Museum in 1915.

4 St Multose

Leave the Kinsale Regional Museum by turning right onto Market Square, which goes uphill and turns into Church Square and you will see St Multose ahead of you on your left. This much-altered Norman church was begun in 1190 and was once the heart of the medieval town. Named after the sixth-century patron saint of Kinsale, it replaces a church which also dated to the sixth century. Romanesque in style, it underwent many changes over the centuries but several original features still survive, including its impressive bell tower. Major reconstruction took place in the nineteenth century when both the floor and roof were renewed. The interior contains some rather fine stained-glass windows, and there is also a large flat stone carved with a round-handed figure traditionally rubbed by fishermen's wives to bring their husbands safely home. Witness to a number of historic moments, the lines scoring the stone at the entrance show how the church was attacked by battering ram. The graveyard is atmospheric and where you can find some of the graves of those who died on the *Lusitania*, the liner sunk off the Old Head of Kinsale in 1915.

DID YOU KNOW?

Prince Rupert declared Charles II King of England in St Multose in 1649. The king's father, Charles I, had been executed during the English Civil War, but his son had to wait until the Restoration in 1660 before being able to return to England and reign.

5 Municipal Hall

Leave St Multose by turning right onto Church Square, then take a right onto Guardwell and a further right onto Higher O'Connell Street and follow it until it turns into Lower O'Connell Street at the junction with Market Quay (on your left). Take the laneway to the right after this junction. This will wind to the left and the right before opening out onto Rampart Lane, where it meets The Mall. Turn left and you will come to Municipal Hall on your left on The Mall. This Gothic castle-like structure is home to Kinsale Town Council and overlooks **The Green**, one of the few places within the old city walls where it was possible to play sport. Used mainly as a bowling green, it is now a pretty little park overlooked by the two-storey stone Municipal Hall, whose symmetrical façade contains projecting bays at either end, giving it the effect of a castle with towers at either end; this is further reinforced by the rows of battlements along the roofline.

6 Kinsale Harbour

Retrace your steps down The Mall, back onto Rampart Lane and down the laneway that zig-zags to Lower O'Connell Street. Then turn left and veer to the right down Market Quay which turns into **Main Street**, full of interesting shops and some good bars, cafés and restaurants. Take the first right and you will come out at the **Town Park**, a small square-shaped green space overlooking Kinsale Harbour. Here you will find the **1916 Memorial** commissioned by the Kinsale History Society to commemorate locals who participated in Ireland's struggle for independence. **Kinsale Harbour** is usually full of boats. Pleasure craft of all sorts dock here. Along the busy waterside you will see the **Spanish Galleon Main Mast** sculpture, a replica of one of the Spanish ships that came to Kinsale in 1601 to support the native Irish

Main Street

chieftains in their doomed struggle against the English. King Philip III of Spain was supporting the Irish in the hopes that it would distract the English from supporting the Dutch in their attempt to throw off Spanish rule in the Netherlands. A force of 6,000 Spaniards set out for Kinsale but bad weather broke up the fleet and only about two thirds arrived. Sadly, the most experienced soldiers (and most of their ammunition) never made it. Ireland's chieftains lost the Battle of Kinsale, altering the course of Irish history. Spain went on to be defeated by the Dutch in the Netherlands (which then went on to become one of the world's richest countries in the seventeenth century – while Spain entered a decline it never really recovered from). For a good way to see the harbour, go on a **Kinsale Harbour Cruise**, one of the town's most popular tourist attractions, and highly recommended, as it is a lovely way to combine history and relaxation and take in some breathtaking scenery.

KINSALE HARBOUR CRUISE

Opening times: Daily, 12 noon – 1 p.m., 2 – 6 p.m.

Admission charges

Kinsale

7 Charles Fort

Charles Fort is located about 3km (2 miles) outside Kinsale. You can follow the signposted **Scilly Walk**, which follows the coast from Long Quay via Lower Road and is one of the nicest such walks in Ireland. It can be busy. Parents particularly like to take little ones on this route as the smooth pedestrian-only path makes it ideal for scooters, bikes and tricycles, and although it is beside the water, it is separated by a wall, making it safe for children to roam ahead without cause for concern. As the road winds out along the coast there are spectacular views of Kinsale Harbour. Pass the well-known pub **The Spaniard**, its name a reminder of the rich history of the town and the legacy left behind, and continue further along the coast road to the beautiful village of **Summercove**. Steep narrow streets are lined with charming whitewashed houses with pretty window shutters. On a sunny day one could imagine oneself in a Greek village instead of in the south of Ireland. The main road is so narrow that two cars cannot pass each other, and the residents are generally good-natured about having to reverse up or down the hill to let one another pass. Although there are no shops in Summercove, there is a fantastic pub called **The Bulman**, popular with tourists and locals alike. In summer, crowds gather outside and across the road, perching on the wall by the water and enjoying late evening sunshine and the stunning view of Kinsale Harbour across the water, while in winter its open fire is cosy.

At the end of Scilly Walk you will come to **Charles Fort**, one of the largest fortresses in the country and one of the finest

••

DID YOU KNOW?

Soldiers stationed at Charles Fort would take local girls to Featherbed Lane, for various reasons. Later on, when their liaisons were ending, the girls would find themselves taken to Heartbreak Hill instead.

remaining examples of a star-shaped bastion fort in the whole of Europe. Paired with James Fort across the estuary, which it superseded, it was built in the 1670s. It seems hard to believe that this peaceful-looking place, with its serene setting and gorgeous views of Kinsale and its harbour, has been the scene of some of Ireland's most brutal and momentous events. Built on the site of an earlier coastal fortification called Ringcurran Castle, it was named for Charles II and remained operational until the 1920s. It protected the town from threats from the sea but proved no match for William of Orange after the Battle of the Boyne in 1690. It remained a British fortress until Ireland's independence in 1922, after which much of it fell into ruin. Declared a National Monument in 1973, it was partially restored and is now open to the public. About 180m (590 feet) to the north-east of the fort is **Trinity Well** on Fort Hill. Derelict for a century, it was restored a few years ago and rededicated by local clergy. Local people have reinstated the old religious practice of walking clockwise (doing the 'rounds') around the well as a way of doing penance, or asking for a special wish.

CHARLES FORT

Opening times: Daily, 10 a.m. – 6 p.m.
(mid March to October),
10 a.m. – 5 p.m.
(November to mid March)
Admission charges
(free entry on first
Wednesday of the month)

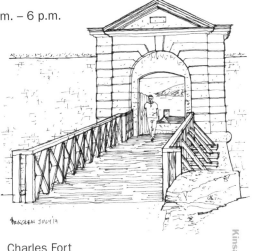

Charles Fort

DID YOU KNOW?

Charles Fort is supposedly haunted by the White Lady of Kinsale, Governor Warrender's daughter, Wilful, who fell in love with one of the soldiers. They got married and went for a stroll on their wedding night. Wilful spotted some flowers and the sentry on duty offered to climb down and pick them for her, if her husband would stand in for him. It took longer than expected and the groom fell asleep and got shot by a commander furious at this dereliction of duty. When Wilful learnt what happened she threw herself off the ramparts, still in her white wedding dress.

8 James Fort

To get to James Fort, leave Kinsale via Pier Road, which turns into the R600. Cross the bridge over the Bandon River and turn left and you will come to this pentagonal fort overlooking the river. James Fort lies opposite Charles Fort at the mouth of Kinsale Harbour. Designed by Paul Ive, construction begun in 1602 (immediately after the Battle of Kinsale) and was completed by 1607. It protected the town and harbour from attack by sea but fell into disuse after Charles Fort was built on the other side of the estuary in the 1670s. It is possible to stroll around the ruins, and on a clear day it makes for a wonderful spot to picnic. The less showy of the two forts, and unlike the busier Charles Fort, James Fort is generally quiet, with just the odd dog walker. It definitely has a desolate beauty all its own, as well as unrivalled views of the harbour and beyond. At the base of the fort lies the popular **Dock Beach**, a lovely sandy strand and a popular place with locals on sunny days.

9 9/11 Garden of Remembrance

Located just off the R600, and best reached by car, is the 9/11 Garden of Remembrance at Ringfinnan. Marked by a striking red wooden gate, a simple plaque reads 'We Will Never Forget'. This is a memorial dedicated to the memory of Fr Michael Judge (chaplain of the New York Fire Department) and 343 of the brave firemen who died so heroically in the line of duty when New York's Twin Towers were destroyed by terrorists on 11 September 2001. Established by Kathleen Murphy on her land, she had spent the last 40 years of her life working as a nurse in New York and was a personal friend of Fr Judge. She wanted to provide a lasting memorial so planted a tree for every one of them. The memorial has been visited by family members and friends who have come to pay respects to their loved ones. The garden itself is a tranquil place of beauty, situated in a place of peaceful isolation. Wandering the aisles of trees, each one tagged with the name of a firefighter, the beautiful vistas of the rolling hillside makes it a very special place to slow down and reflect on the bravery of those who lost their lives. Kathleen herself died in 2011 after a battle with cancer – a simple stone monument commemorates her life.

10 Lusitania Museum

The Lusitania Museum is housed in the Old Head Signal Tower located on the R604 about 12km (7.5 miles) from Kinsale. This is best reached by car. In 1796 Wolfe Tone and the United Irishmen led a French army in an attempt to land at Bantry Bay. Bad weather thwarted the invasion, but the attack, combined with local political unrest, greatly alarmed the British. Fearful of another maritime attack from Napoleonic France through England's 'back door' of Ireland, they built a series of defensive watchtowers on vulnerable stretches of Irish coastline. Between 1804 and 1806, 81 signal towers, Martello towers and batteries were built within sight of each

THE *LUSITANIA*

The *Lusitania* was a British passenger liner operated by the Cunard Line. Launched in 1906, it made a total of 202 transatlantic crossings before being torpedoed by a German submarine on 7 May 1915. Because it was travelling so fast it was not possible to launch the lifeboats immediately and it sank in under twenty minutes, killing 1,198 of the 1,962 passengers and crew on board. The First World War was brutal, but the targeting of innocent civilians was considered a shocking outrage, and because 128 of them were American, this shifted public opinion in the United States against Germany, a factor in the United States joining the Allies in 1917 and instrumental in their winning the war the following year.

other. Starting in Dublin from the Pigeon House Fort, they wound their way along the east and south coasts. The **Old Head Signal Tower** was number 25. Using a flag-and-ball signalling system, messages could be sent from one tower to the next and on a clear day a signal leaving Bantry Bay was said to be able to reach Dublin Castle in two hours. The newly restored Old Head Signal Tower is situated at the highest point of the scenic Old Head peninsula. A Lusitania Memorial Garden opened in 2017, and a 20m (65-foot) bronze wave sculpted by Liam Lavery and Eithne Ring commemorates the ship's tragic final voyage. The ground floor of the signal tower is devoted to the history of signal towers, while the first floor houses the **Lusitania Museum**. There is a scale model of the liner as well as items recovered from the wreck, including a brass filigree window from the first-class deck area. The parapet walkway is accessible from the internal stairs on the first floor where panoramic views of the Seven Heads Peninsula take in the Old Head Lighthouse, as well as the nearby Garrettstown and Garrylucas beaches, Courtmacsherry Bay, Charles Fort and Kinsale Harbour.

LUSITANIA MUSEUM
Opening times: Daily, 10 a.m. – 6 p.m. (March to October)
Admission charges

11 Old Head of Kinsale

The Old Head of Kinsale is located about 15km (9 miles) south-west of Kinsale at the end of the R604 and best reached by car. This is a particularly picturesque stretch of rugged coastline. The headland juts 3km (2.8 miles) into the Atlantic Ocean with dramatic cliffs that rise as high as 90m (300 feet). The cliffs offer protected breeding grounds for many species of birds, including kittiwake, peregrines and guillemot, and whales and dolphins can often be spotted further out to sea. The exclusive 18-hole **Old Head Golf Links** opened in 1997 and not only boasts spectacular views but has been played by both President Bill Clinton and Tiger Woods. Huge controversy surrounded the development of the golf course and it was bitterly contested by locals, environmentalists and nature lovers. Cork County Council and An Bord Pleanála fought for public right of access to be granted through the land, but this was overruled by the Supreme Court.

ARCHITECTURAL STYLES

This section is alphabetically arranged to explain briefly some of the architectural styles mentioned in the book, particularly two of its most important, Neoclassical and Gothic. Towards the end of the nineteenth century there was a new spirit of eclecticism in Irish architecture and a number of different styles began to flourish. Some of them were a return to older styles, particularly those from the pre-industrial era, which took on a romantic hue through all that nineteenth-century grit and smoke – the Arts and Crafts style sought to re-establish artisanal craftsmanship, while others, like Byzantine or Romanesque, made specific reference to long-vanished eras. In the twentieth century there was a new departure, stylistically, with the streamlined Art Deco and the even more stripped-down Modernism that followed it making their presence felt. Postmodernism briefly reared its colourful head in the 1980s and 1990s. This chapter ends with a look at some more recent architectural development in 21st-century Ireland under the heading Contemporary.

Architecture in Ireland

I RELAND IS AN ANCIENT ISLAND, one with a rich and varied architectural heritage. Yet the country has also had a long and turbulent history, with numerous invasions and rebellions. The oldest surviving buildings on the island reflect this with Iron Age stone forts (known as 'raths', a word you will find in many Irish place names) enclosed by earthen banks, a timber fence and a ditch. People lived in huts inside these fortifications and had underground storage (which doubled up as a refuge when needed). The Christianisation of Ireland ushered in a golden age, with numerous monasteries and churches being built in the Romanesque style. This was where monks kept the light of learning aglow in a continent experiencing the depths of the Dark Ages. From the eighth century onwards Irish monks made their way across Europe, rekindling knowledge that might otherwise have been lost. It was not all sweetness and light, however, because back in Ireland the Vikings had begun to make vicious raids, yet the Irish people continued to live, and thrive, if the round towers they built in this era are anything to judge by. Sometimes more than 30m (100 feet) high, these simple yet elegant structures were built during the tenth and twelfth centuries as part of monastic sites as their bell towers. The entrance was usually high off the ground, but this was for structual reasons. Often as high as 4m (13 feet), they were reached by wooden staircases. These have not survived, but traces of them can still be found.

Even the Vikings did not just pillage and burn, they also established settlements along the south and east coasts of the country from the ninth century onwards, notably Waterford, Wexford and Dublin, but their buildings were made of wood and have long since vanished. Churches and monasteries tended to be made of stone and over the centuries the heavy Romanesque style gave way to a lighter Gothic. When the Anglo-Normans invaded in the twelfth century they built stone castles, like Barryscourt, which were strong and easily defended. The native chieftains did the same (Blarney Castle is a good example). The seventeenth century was one of conflict, both in the 1640s, when Cromwell ravaged the country, and in the late 1680s and early 1690s, when there was a power struggle between the Catholic King James II and his (ultimately successful) Dutch rival, Prince William of Orange, who became King William III. One of the stylistic legacies of this era was the introduction of Dutch-style gables. Not many of these remain, although a few can still be seen dotted around Cork city and even in Kinsale (the Regional Museum).

The eighteenth century was one of peace and prosperity and ushered in a second golden age for Ireland. While in Cork none of the elegant residential squares were built that are such an ornament to Georgian Dublin, some fine, gracious streets, like South Mall, were laid out. Ireland entered into something of a decline again in the nineteenth century. Parliament dissolved itself in 1801 (making the country part of the United Kingdom), and then there was the disastrous Great Famine of the 1840s, yet building continued, some of it quite decorative and often harking back to past eras. The Gothic style was particularly popular for churches, schools and convents (and plenty of these were built after Catholic Emancipation in 1829, although church building for Catholics had started as far back as the 1760s in Cork). The twentieth century saw the introduction of new styles, including Art Deco, which started in Paris (a number of buildings on St Patrick Street are in this style). Later came the Modern Movement, a rather severe and undecorated style, followed briefly by Postmodernism, an eclectic reaction to the austerity of high Modernism, and by the end of the twentieth century there was a return to simpler forms, with elegant new buildings built in a style that we can call Contemporary.

Art Deco

One of the most important cultural events of the 1920s was the *Exposition des Arts Décoratifs et Industriels Modernes* held in Paris in 1925. Known as Art Deco, this resulted in the world's last total design movement, meaning that its streamlined elegance could be applied just as easily to a cigarette lighter as a luxury liner, an apartment building or the piano in its penthouse. It was also the first truly global style, expressing the aspirations and technical capabilities of the modern age. Art Deco was particularly popular with commercial buildings, and a number of the larger shops on St Patrick Street are in this style. An excellent example would be Debenham's (originally built as Roches Stores).

Arts and Crafts

This movement, born out of the Gothic style, was widely influential in the late nineteenth century. It attempted to re-establish skills and craftsmanship that were being lost to industrialisation and mass production. Popularised through the writings of Pugin and Ruskin, it was William Morris who took the most practical steps to

Beamish and Crawford (former) stables, Bishop Street

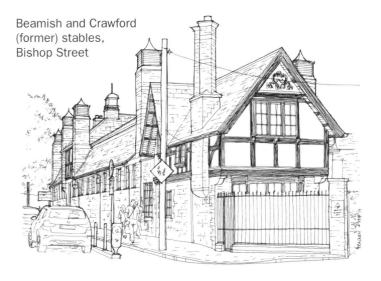

re-establish industries along medieval manufacturing lines that would retain truth to materials and make use of construction methods that adhered to the function and essence of their design. The Oval on South Main Street, nearly opposite the old Beamish and Crawford brewery, is an excellent example of this charming style, as is the brewery's former stables on Proby's Quay (see p. 161).

Byzantine

This style takes its name from the Byzantine Empire, the eastern half of the Roman Empire, which continued for a thousand years after the western half had fallen to the Barbarians. Established in what is modern-day Turkey, the Emperor Constantine moved his capital from Rome to Byzantium in 306 AD and renamed it Constantinople. It remained the capital of the Byzantine Empire until it was reconquered by the Turks in 1453. (The name Constantinople was changed to Istanbul in 1919.) Byzantine architecture is sumptuous and heady, as befits its oriental origins. It makes use of luxurious materials, like marble and mosaic, as well as rich colours. One of its characteristic motifs is the use of the round dome over a square base. Concave triangular supports, known as squinches, enable the dome to fit over the square plan. An impressive example of this style is St Francis's church on Liberty Street.

Contemporary

Along with Ireland's new-found wealth at the end of the twentieth century came a confidence in Irish art, architecture and design. Irish architects have become well-respected abroad in a way not seen since the nineteenth century, and some of their work is being held up as an example of tasteful, appropriate contemporary design. New-found wealth also meant new funding for architectural projects,

Lewis Glucksman
Gallery, UCC

yet there have always been some loyal patrons of the arts and architecture in Cork. Religious institutions in particular have given much employment to architects, even in lean times. Another sponsor of conspicuous merit is University College Cork, which not only commissioned the Hiberno-Romanesque masterpiece of the Honan Chapel at the beginning of the twentieth century, it continued its good work in the twenty-first by commissioning the lovely Lewis Glucksman Gallery.

Gothic

This style succeeded the Romanesque and is native to northern
Europe. It began in France (where the most beautiful variant of it,
Rayonnant, can be found). The main aim was to allow as much light
as possible into a building and this led to the replacing of heavy
masonry walls with slender columns, allowing for much larger
windows. Structural innovations such as the flying buttress and
pointed arch also allowed for column-free interiors. Gothic waned
in popularity as the Renaissance took hold and Europe rediscovered
the Ancient World's Classical architecture but it experienced a
strong revival in the nineteenth century, particularly in England and
Ireland. A lovely example of Gothic Revival in Cork is the former
Carmichael School on the corner of MacCurtain Street and
Summerhill.

Carmichael School (former),
Summerhill

Modernism

The Modern Movement was born in the first half of the twentieth century. Developed by the architects Walter Gropius, Ludwig Mies van der Rohe, Le Corbusier and others, it sought to improve society by making people better prepared to meet the challenges of the modern era. They thought the best way to achieve this was to eradicate ornamentation and get rid of any historical references or anything else that might distract the busy citizen from the brisk business of living their lives as efficiently as possible. The style was minimalist, and also embraced innovations from industry. Efficiency and hygiene were its watchwords as 'machines for living' were built. Also known as the International Style, Modernist buildings invariably used reinforced-concrete frames and had vast areas of glass. Their interiors were uncluttered. It was popular for mid-twentieth-century skyscrapers. Sadly, it was also the style of choice for designers of social housing after the Second World War and came to be criticised for being much too sterile (as well as unresponsive to local context). The City Library on Grand Parade is in the Modernist style.

Neoclassicism

Classical architecture flowered in ancient Greece and Rome in the centuries before and after the birth of Christ. As a style it was elegant and harmonious but it disappeared with the fall of the Roman Empire. It was revived in the sixteenth century, first in Italy and then through the rest of Europe, thanks to Andrea Palladio, an Italian architect who studied the ruins of ancient Rome and adapted them to suit his era. Inigo Jones introduced the style to England in the early seventeenth century with his Queen's House, Greenwich, London, and it quickly spread. It makes use of five classical orders: Doric, Ionic, Corinthian, Tuscan and Composite. Beginning in

Greece in the fifth century BC, and adapted by the Romans, the five orders have been the cornerstone of Neoclassical architecture ever since. It reached a height of popularity in Ireland and England in the eighteenth century when the Italian country villa, as perfected by Palladio, was used as the basis for some of the era's finest stately homes (such as Russborough House in County Wicklow). It was used extensively in Cork: the Cork Savings Bank on Lapp's Quay is a magnificent example. It was also used for domestic dwellings, at least for those who could afford them. The Georgian houses on South Mall are fine examples of this restrained and elegant style.

Postmodernism

Postmodernism was a reaction to the austerity of Modernism. It emerged in the 1970s and became extremely fashionable in the 1980s and early 1990s. It made eclectic use of motifs such as the ancient Classical orders, columns, capitals and cornices, often quite crudely, or in an attempt to be witty. Like any movement conceived as a reaction to something else, it failed to coalesce and its practitioners remained too individualistic to allow it to cohere into a long-lasting style. It quickly spilt into a number of different camps, two of the best known being High-Tech and Deconstructivism.

Romanesque

This style was popular in Western Europe from the seventh to the twelfth centuries, a time when major structures were either castles or churches. Walls were thick and windows small, with round-headed arches. The style still contained some features of the ancient Classical world, such as capitals derived from late Roman or Byzantine models, but these were coarsened and rather crude-

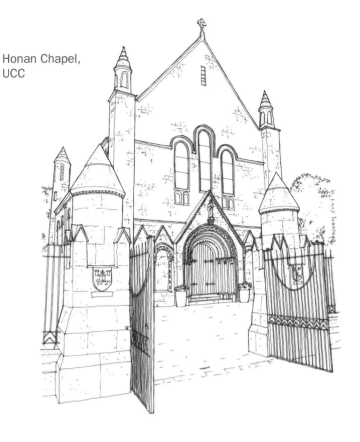

Honan Chapel,
UCC

looking and bore little relation to the originals. The Honan Chapel
at UCC is a very fine example of what is known as Hiberno-
Romanesque, a scholarly Irish revival of the Romanesque style that
took hold from the end of the nineteenth century onwards.

Adam style (and Adamesque): style of Neoclassicism popularised by the brothers Robert and James Adam in the eighteenth century noted for its uniform interiors.

Apse: a recess, usually semicircular, projecting from an external wall.

Arcade: a long arched gallery or veranda, often open at only one side, formed by a series of arches supported by columns or piers.

Arch: curved structure over opening.

Art Deco: style in art and architecture popular in the 1920s and 1930s that drew inspiration from industrial elements.

Art Nouveau: style that flourished from the 1880s to the outbreak of the First World War characterised by sinuous lines and asymmetry.

Arts and Crafts: late nineteenth-century English movement that sought to re-establish traditional craftsmanship as a response to increasing industrialisation.

Ashlar: square blocks of neatly cut and finished stone.

Attic: a storey over the main entablature.

Baluster: upright support in a balustrade.

Balustrade: a row of balusters supporting a handrail.

Battlement: parapet with alternating higher and lower parts originally used for defence.

Bawn: walled enclosure often protected by towers.

Bay window: a window that projects from a building.

Belfry: a bell tower.

Breakfront: an element that stands out from a building's façade.

Buttress: projecting wall support.

Byzantine: style associated with the Byzantine Empire (AD 306–1453).

Capital: head or topmost part of a column or pillar, often ornamental.

Carrera marble: marble from the famous Carrera quarries in Italy.

Castellated: with battlements.

Chancel: the part of a church containing the altar and sanctuary and often the choir.

Choir: in larger churches, the place reserved for the choir or singers, sometimes screened.

Clerestory: upper part of walls carried on arcades or colonnades in a church, higher than the external lean-to roofs, pierced with windows to allow in light.

Cloister: an enclosed court attached to a monastery.

Colonnade: row of columns.

Column: a supporting element, always round in shape.

Corinthian order: the third of the Greek orders and fourth of the Roman; decorative, slender and elegant with two rows of acanthus leaves sprouting volutes or small scrolls.

Cornice: the top part of an entablature.

Cupola: small dome.

Curtain wall: straight wall between castle towers; thin, non-loadbearing external wall.

Diocletian window: semicircular window, usually divided into three vertical compartments.

Dome: a vaulted circular roof or ceiling.

Doric order: Classical order of architecture with distinct Greek and Roman varieties; simple in style, the Roman is less squat looking than the Greek, always fluted but invariably without a base.

Dormer window: window projecting from a roof with its own roof.

Dungeon: prison cell usually located in the basement of a castle keep.

Edwardian: British architectural style in the first decade of the twentieth century, invariably ornate.

Engaged column: a column attached to a wall.

Entablature: an entire horizontal band carried on columns or pillars.

Faience: a type of glazed terracotta.

Frieze: horizontal central band of Classical entablature, below the cornice and above the architrave.

Gable: triangular upper part of a wall at the end of a roof.

Georgian: British and Irish architecture during the reign of Kings George I–IV (1715–1830), predominantly Neoclassical in style.

Gothic: style of architecture in Western Europe from the twelfth to the sixteenth century; its main features were pointed arches, buttresses and delicately carved stonework.

Gothic Revival: a nineteenth-century rediscovery of the Gothic style.

Hiberno-Romanesque: style of religious building in Ireland from the tenth to the twelfth century characterised by simple rectangular buildings with detached circular towers, it was revived at the end of the nineteenth century as part of the Arts and Crafts movement during Ireland's Celtic Revival.

In antis: usually used to describe a portico that is recessed within a structure instead of projecting from it.

Ionic order: Classical order of architecture, the second in Greek and the third in Roman; easily identified by its capital with rolled-up scrolls; the Greek shafts are invariably fluted.

Italianate: nineteenth-century style of architecture modelled on Italian palazzos.

Kentish ragstone: a hard grey limestone from Kent in the UK.

Lombardo-Romanesque: Romanesque style of architecture originally from eleventh-century Lombardy in Italy, revived in the nineteenth century.

Machicolations: space under a projecting parapet used for throwing defensive missiles.

Mansard roof: a roof with two slopes, the lower one being very steep.

Nave: the main body of a church, the place where the worshippers sit.

Neoclassical: style of architecture popular from the seventeenth century onwards and based on the architecture of ancient Greece and Rome; buildings are usually symmetrical, have elegant proportioning and are characterised by the generous use of columns and pillars.

Octastyle: a portico with eight columns or pillars.

Oriel window: a bay window projecting from an upper storey.

Palazzo: an Italian palace.

Palladian: in the style of sixteenth-century Italian architect Andrea Palladio who revived ancient Roman building styles and typologies.

Palladian window: a tripartite window with an arch over the central part (also known as a serliana).

Pilaster: an upright rectangular pier that looks like a pillar attached to a wall.

Pillar: a supporting element, always square in shape.

Plinth: plain continuous projecting surface under the base-mounting of a wall, pedestal or podium; the low plain block under a column or pillar in Classical architecture.

Portico: roof supported by columns or pillars, usually forming an entrance.

Postmodern: a decorative and eclectic style that began in the 1970s as a reaction to the starkness of Modernism.

Queen Anne: an understated and well-proportioned Neoclassicism popular during the reign of Queen Anne (1702–14), it featured red brick and sash windows.

Quoin: stone on a building's corner.

Rath: the Irish word for a fort.

Rayonnant: Gothic style of architecture popular in France in the thirteenth and fourteenth centuries, it takes its name from the shapes made by tracery bars in the windows and the radiating rib vaults.

Regency: style of architecture popular from the 1790s to the 1820s (when George IV acted as Regent for his father George III).

Renaissance: a revival of ancient Classical humanism that began in Italy in the fourteenth century and spread through Europe.

Render: a finishing surface applied to a building, often plaster.

Retardataire: any style of architecture that looks old-fashioned when it is built.

Rib vault: type of vault created where two or three barrel vaults intersect.

Romanesque: architectural style in Europe from the seventh to the twelfth centuries characterised by heavy stone masonry, small round windows and doors and coarsened Classical decorative features.

Roughcast: type of rough plasterwork, often incorporating pebbles, used for building exteriors.

Rose window: a circular window popular in Gothic architecture, especially in larger churches or cathedrals, usually subdivided by complex radial tracery to form a floral pattern.

Rotunda: building or room shaped like a cylinder.

Rustication: stone cut so that the joints are sunk in a channel.

Sacristy: store room in a church for garments and utensils.

Scagliola: imitation marble made of crushed gypsum and then coloured, in use since Antiquity and popular during the seventeenth and eighteenth centuries.

Scottish Baronial: nineteenth-century architectural style influenced by the castles of Scotland featuring battlements, turrets, and conical roofs.

Squinch: a small arch spanning the corner angle between walls.

Stuccadore: a plasterer.

Terracotta: hard unglazed pottery used in decorative tiles, urns and statuary.

Tempietto: Small Renaissance-style temple, often circular.

Transept: any large division at right angles to the main body of a building (especially a church).

Triforia: plural of triforium, an upper-floor aisle with its own arcade on the interior of a church's nave, often seen in Romanesque and Gothic architecture.

Tudor: style of architecture developed between the reigns of Henry VII (begun 1485) and Elizabeth I (died 1603) which saw the introduction of Renaissance-style decoration.

Turret: a small tower normally forming part of a larger structure.

Tuscan order: one of the five Roman orders, simplest and undecorated.

Victorian: style of architecture during the reign of Queen Victoria (1837–1901), invariably highly decorative.

William and Mary: a plain but elegant architectural style named after King William III and Queen Mary II which was popular from 1690 to 1715. It incorporated Dutch elements, like gables and large windows.

GENERAL

Cork Heritage
www.corkheritage.ie

Cork City Tourist Office
Tel: 021 425 5100
www.corkcity.ie

SHANDON

St Mary and St Anne's Cathedral
Tel: 021 430 4325

St Anne's Shandon
Tel: 021 450 5906
www.shandonbells.ie

Cork Butter Museum
Tel: 021 430 0600
www.corkbutter.museum

Shandon Craft Centre
Tel: 021 450 3936

Firkin Crane Theatre
Tel: 021 450 7487
www.firkincrane.ie

Cork Civic Trust
Tel: 021 421 5101
www.civictrusthouse.ie

Cork Arts Theatre
Tel: 021 450 5624
www.corkartstheatre.com

Murphy Heineken Brewery
Tel: 021 450 3371
www.heinekenireland.ie

MACCURTAIN STREET TO CITY HALL

Everyman Theatre
Tel: 021 450 1673
www.everymancork.com

Metropole Hotel
Tel: 021 464 3700
www.themetropolehotel.ie

Tigh Filí
Tel: 021 421 5175

Trinity Presbyterian Church
Tel: 021 489 1437

St Patrick's
Tel: 021 450 2696
www.stpatrickscork.com

Sculpture Factory
Tel: 021 431 4353
www.nationalsculpturefactory.com

The Elysian
www.theelysian.ie

City Hall
Tel: 021 496 6222
www.corkcity.ie

Charlie's
Tel: 021 431 8342
www.charliesbarcork.com

SOUTH MALL AND OLIVER PLUNKETT STREET

Imperial Hotel
Tel: 021 427 4040

The Hi-B Bar
Tel: 021 427 2758

The Long Valley
Tel: 021 427 2144
www.thelongvalleybar.com

ST PATRICK'S STREET AND ENVIRONS

Debenham's
Tel: 1890 946 779
www.debenhams.ie

Brown Thomas
Tel: 021 480 5555
www.brownthomas.com

Cork Opera House
Tel: 021 427 0022
www.corkoperahouse.ie

Crawford Art Gallery
Tel: 021 480 5042
www.crawfordartgallery.ie

Half Moon Theatre
Tel: 021 427 1160

Ss Peter and Paul's
Tel: 021 427 6573
www.saintspeterandpauls.org

Waterstone's
Tel: 021 427 6522
www.waterstones.com

The Woodford
Tel: 021 425 3931
www.thewoodford.ie

Dennehy's
Tel: 021 427 2343

GRAND PARADE

English Market
www.englishmarket.ie

Farmgate Café
Tel: 021 427 8134
www.farmgate.ie

City Library
Tel: 021 492 4900
www.corkcitylibraries.ie

The Electric
Tel: 021 422 2990
www.electriccork.ie

HOLY TRINITY TO ST FIN BARRE'S CATHEDRAL

Holy Trinity Church
www.holytrinity.irishcapuchins.com

Nano Nagle Place
Tel: 021 419 3580
www.nanonagleplace.ie

Tom Barry's
Tel: 021 431 8498

Elizabeth Fort
Tel: 021 497 5947

St Fin Barre's Cathedral
Tel: 021 496 3387
www.corkcathedral.webs.com

MEDIEVAL CITY

The Oval
Tel: 021 427 8952

Masonic Hall
Tel: 021 427 4095
www.munsterfreemason.com

Triskel Christchurch
Tel: 021 427 2022
www.triskelartscentre.ie

St Augustine's
Tel: 021 427 0410
www.staugustinescork.ie

St Peter's (former)
Tel: 021 427 8187
www.stpeterscork.ie

Granary Theatre
Tel: 021 490 4275
www.granary@ucc.ie

UNIVERSITY COLLEGE CORK
TO SUNDAY'S WELL

University College Cork
Tel: 021 490 1876
www.ucc.ie

Lewis Glucksman Gallery
Tel: 021 490 1844
www.glucksman.org

Honan Chapel
Tel: 021 490 3088
www.honanchapel.com

Fitzgerald Park
Tel: 021 492 4000
www.corkcity.ie

Cork Public Museum
Tel: 021 427 0679
www.corkcity.ie

Vertigo
Tel: 021 485 6610

Cork City Gaol
Tel: 021 430 5022
www.corkcitygaol.com

FURTHER AFIELD

Old Cork Waterworks
Tel: 021 494 1500
www.lifetimelab.ie

Blarney Castle
Tel: 021 438 5252
www.blarneycastle.ie

Blackrock Castle
Tel: 021 435 7917
www.bco.ie

Fota House and Gardens
Tel: 021 481 5543
www.fotahouse.com

Fota Wildlife Park
Tel: 021 481 2678
www.fotawildlife.ie

Ballyvolane House
Tel: 025 36349
www.ballyvolanehouse.ie

Ballymaloe House
Tel: 021 465 2531
www.ballymaloe.ie

COBH

General
www.visitcobh.com

Cobh Road Train
Tel: 086 338 1237
www.cobhroadtrain.com

Cobh Heritage Centre
Tel: 021 481 3591
www.cobhheritage.com

Genealogical Family History Research Profile
Tel: 021 481 3591
Email: genealogy@cobhheritage.com

Cobh Museum
Tel: 021 481 4240
www.cobhmuseum.com

Cork Harbour Boat Hire
Tel: 086 074 7926
Email:
sales@corkharbourboathire.com

Sirius Arts Centre
Tel: 021 481 3790
www.siriusartscentre.ie

Commodore Hotel
Tel: 021 481 1277
www.commodorehotel.ie

Titanic Experience
Tel: 021 481 4412
www.titanicexperiencecobh.ie

The Titanic Trail
Tel: 087 276 7218
www.titanic.ie

Cobh Tourist Office
Tel: 481 3301
www.cobhharbourchamber.ie

St Colman's Cathedral
Tel: 021 481 3222
www.cobhcathedralparish.ie

St Benedict's Priory
Tel: 021 481 1448

Spike Island
Tel: 085 851 8818
www.spikeislandcork.ie

KINSALE

Kinsale Tourist Office
Tel: 021 477 2234
www.kinsale.ie

Dermot Ryan's Kinsale Heritage Town Walks
Tel: 021 477 2729

Don and Barry's Historic Stroll
Tel: 087 250 0731
www.historicstrollkinsale.com

Perryville House
Tel: 021 477 2731
www.perryvillehouse.com

Kinsale Regional Museum
Tel: 021 477 7930

Desmond Castle / International Museum of Wine
Tel: 021 477 4855

Kinsale Harbour Cruise
Tel: 086 250 5456
www.kinsaleharbourcruises.com

The Spaniard
Tel: 021 477 2436

The Bulman
Tel: 021 477 2131
www.thebulman.ie

Charles Fort
Tel: 021 477 2263

James Fort
Tel: 021 477 2234

INDEX